THE DUTIES

AND

LIABILITIES OF TRUSTEES

SIX LECTURES

DELIVERED IN THE INNER TEMPLE DURING THE
HILARY SITTINGS, 1896, AT THE REQUEST OF
THE COUNCIL OF LEGAL EDUCATION

BY

AUGUSTINE BIRRELL

ONE OF HIS MAJESTY'S COUNSEL

MACMILLAN AND CO., LIMITED
ST. MARTIN'S STREET, LONDON
1920

PREFACE

THESE Lectures were delivered at the request of the Council of Legal Education, and are now printed at the request of a good many people who did not hear them.

I have only a word to say by way of preface. My learned friends in Lincoln's Inn with whom it has been my happiness to associate for twenty years, have no concern with this little volume. Courageous as they already are in their attack upon a Trustee, and wily (if retained on his behalf) in his defence, what is there for me, of all men, to teach my brethren? Nothing whatever.

My sole object has been, and I shall be sorry if I have wholly failed to effect it, to bring out in bold relief the plain duties and the equally plain, but none the less disagreeable, liabilities of express Trustees, in such a manner as to engage the attention alike of the student of our law, and of the many men and women, who, though not lawyers, are yet Trustees.

In considering the provisions of the recent Trustee Act of 1893, I have found an edition of that Act edited with notes by my two learned friends, Mr. Rudall and Mr. J. W. Greig, and published by Jordan and Sons of Chancery Lane, price six shillings net, most useful and trust-worthy.   A. B.

3, New Square,
  Lincoln's Inn

CONTENTS

FIRST LECTURE.

FOURTH LECTURE.

FIFTH LECTURE.

SIXTH LECTURE.

THE DUTIES

AND

LIABILITIES OF TRUSTEES

THE DUTIES

AND

LIABILITIES OF TRUSTEES

I

My distinguished predecessor in this place, for chair I must not call it, Mr. Willis, was luckier than I in his choice of a subject, for abstruse though the law of negotiable securities may be, it has this advantage over my unwieldy theme—it has been made the subject matter of scientific legislation.

The whole law was embodied in a Bill carefully drafted by a most accomplished lawyer; this Bill was submitted to

E   B

revision by select committees of both
Houses of Parliament, and then passed
into Law without amendment or murmur.
After a decent interval the draftsman was
made a County Court judge. There are
things even in this world which are
exactly what they should be.

The student though he will not be able
without much reading to comprehend the
full significance of the one hundred
clauses of 45 and 46 of the Queen, chap-
ter 61, intituled "An Act to codify the
law relating to Bills of Exchange, Cheques
and Promissory Notes," yet has the
satisfaction, and in legal matters it is a
very real satisfaction, of knowing that
with the statute kept open before him he
is not likely to overlook or be unmindful
of anything it really behoves him to
remember.

How different is my plight. My subject, *The Duties and Liabilities of
Trustees*, is still at large in the library,

where it lurks in volumes of reports to be
counted by hundreds, or lies buried, but
with a hideous power of inopportune
resurrection, in some partially repealed
statute.

It is terribly easy not only to overlook or (speaking frankly) to be ignorant
of a case, but to forget an Act of Parliament.

Towards the end of last sittings and
almost at the close of a case relating to
Trustees then being tried in the Chancery
division, it became apparent from an
observation made from the bench that all
the four counsel engaged in the case,
learned and experienced men as they
were, had not considered the provisions
of the most recent Trustee Act, that of
1894, though such provisions bore directly
upon the subject matter.

I advise the young practitioner which-
ever volume of the Law Reports he may
choose to neglect, not to let it be the one

containing the statutes. Nobody knows
what goes on in Parliament—our laws
are reformed in the dead of night in
silence and obscurity—yet none the less
are these statutes, unless wholly unintelli-
gible, binding alike upon the most head-
strong and self-opinionative of County
Court judges, and upon those sublimer
beings who, regardless of authority, occupy the scarlet benches of the House of
Lords.

But if I am oppressed by the difficulty
of my subject, I am encouraged both by
its importance and its personal interest.

I am addressing those who are or who
hope shortly to become lawyers; in other
words I am addressing those who are
already or are almost certain to become
Trustees.

Here I have an advantage over Mr.
Willis, and I must make the most of it.
I have never, nervous and timid man
that I am, drawn a bill, or accepted a bill,

or endorsed a bill, and unless I strangely
misread my destiny, I shall never do any
of these things ; but despite his nervous-
ness and timidity, the unhappy being
who addresses you is the legal personal representative of nine deceased persons and
the Trustee of five marriage settlements.

It is our fate ; we can hardly hope to
resist it, and therefore to study the subject
becomes if not a pleasant, at all events a
pressing duty. The chart I have to draw
is of waters through which most of you
will have to plough your way.

First, let me make plain the *scope* and
purport of this course of lectures.

I do not propose to inflict upon you
any learning as to uses and trusts before
the Statute 27, Henry VIII. ch. 10, or
after it.

I hope I shall never be guilty of
speaking disrespectfully of our old law,
the ancient learning. I would far sooner
spend an evening or two re-reading

Mr. Sanders' famous essay on *Uses and Trusts*, a treatise rendered delightful by the precision of its language quite apart from the fascination of its theme, than I would lose my time and temper over many of the novels of the day; but it so happens that these lectures of mine as I have planned them do not involve the old law.

I need not do more than remind you of the familiar classes into which trusts are divided, for all this you can more readily read for yourselves in the early pages of Mr. Lewin's now swollen volume, or in Mr. Godefrois' later work.

A trust is a confidence reposed in and accepted by some person or persons, and it is an *Express Trust* when it has been intentionally and deliberately created, as when any one gives away property to another but at the same time declares that such property shall be held or applied in a particular way for the benefit of some person or persons other than the formal donee, or of some other person or persons as well as of the donee. If this transaction is done once for all in a completed form, it is an *Executed Express Trust,* but if it requires to be supplemented by further acts on the part of the creator of the trust, it is called an *Executory Express Trust.*

Implied Trusts are trusts which are inferred by minds trained in equitable doctrines either from language employed during a transaction or from the circumstances which surround the transaction. An Implied Trust gives effect to an intention attributed to the parties.

Resulting and Constructive Trusts are the creatures of equitable rules, and arise by operation of law and have nothing to do with the declarations or supposed wishes of the parties. Examples of these different kinds of trusts are given in all the text books.

Only one other classification need be mentioned—*Public Trusts* and *Private Trusts*. Public Trusts are *Charitable Trusts* and their concerns are supposed to occupy a good deal of the ample and well-paid leisure of Her Majesty's Attorney-General.

With one only of these divers trusts are we concerned, *the Express Executed Private Trust*.

Trusts of this class are created in the vast majority of instances either by will or by deed.

Do not go away and say that I said a deed was necessary to create an express executed private trust. I did not say so. No deed is necessary. A trust of personal estate may be created or declared by word of mouth and proved by parol evidence, and in the case of land any document signed by the creator of the trust containing the terms of the trust and indicating the property over which the trust extends will satisfy the Statute of Frauds.

But for all that I propose to confine your attention, if I am so fortunate as to obtain it, to trusts declared by will or by deed—the deed usually being what is called a marriage settlement.

The Trustees, whose duties and liabilities we are to consider, are those persons who, being appointed Trustees of property by will or by deed, have accepted the office.

Some old friend has died leaving a wife and seven children, the eldest of whom is fifteen the youngest two, and when the will comes to be read, it turns out that the testator has appointed you an executor and Trustee, and has bidden you, after paying his debts and funeral expenses, to stand possessed of the clear residue of his estate upon trust, either to retain it in its then state of investment, or to sell and re-invest in certain specified securities, to receive the income and pay it to the widow during her life, and after her death to divide the trust estate equally amongst such of the children as being boys shall live to attain twenty-one or being girls shall attain that age or marry under it. Well, it does not do to be disagreeable at funerals. The widow, poor thing, takes you apart and after casually mentioning that she has always liked you the best of her husband's friends, tells you how the burden of her sorrows will be lightened if you consent to act. You do consent, and after a glass of sherry and a biscuit, leave the house of your old friend the Trustee of his wife and of his children, and even it may be, of his children's children.

Or possibly your sister is about to marry a man in whom you see no reason to place any unusual degree of confidence. A settlement is proposed of her small fortune—the trusts being the usual trusts of a marriage settlement, and resembling those I have above briefly indicated. You are asked to be a Trustee, —it would be churlish to refuse— you give your consent, the deed is prepared and executed by the necessary parties, the marriage is solemnised, the married couple start for the Riviera or the Isle of Wight, whilst you return to your chambers a Trustee, to find on your table instructions to settle a writ in an action seeking to make some estimable members of the class you have just joined, personally liable to make good a breach of trust.

I have but one other preliminary observation to make, executors and Trustees are often associated, but they are not the same thing. By our law, men who die possessed of property must have either executors appointed by themselves, or administrators appointed by others to carry on their *personæ*, to wind up their affairs, pay their funeral expenses and the

costs of administration, and so ascertain
what (if any) clear residue is left to go
either as disposed of by the will or to the
next of kin according to law. With this
work of adminstration, Trustees as such
have nothing to do. Their duties begin
when the residue has been ascertained,
or when any specific sums to which
under the will they may as Trustees be
entitled, have been handed over to them,
discharged from all liability to meet the
debts and prior obligations of the testator.

The law regulating the conduct of executors and Trustees though similar (for an
executor though not a Trustee is in a fiduciary position) is not identical, their duties
being different. Still I cannot promise
to keep them quite separate all through
these lectures, for though an executor
is not a Trustee *ab initio*, he is very often
appointed a Trustee as well as an executor,
and the precise moment when his duties
as an executor come to an end and his

duties as a Trustee begin is hard to
ascertain. When does he undergo this
rare law change? The late Sir John
Wickens, a very nice observer, used to
tell his pupils that it invariably took
place in the dead hours of the night,
but so close an investigation is to be
deprecated.

And now I think we are fairly afloat.

In the syllabus [1] which, by the kindness
of the council has been printed and cir-
culated, I have referred to important
changes recently made in the law relating
to Trustees by statute, and to a new
temper and disposition shown towards
Trustees by the judges of the High
Court.

Our laws, whether made by judges or
legislators in Parliament assembled, re-
flect more or less tardily and clumsily
men's feelings and opinions. The *Zeit-*

[1] This Syllabus is substantially reproduced in
the Table of Contents.

geist, or Time-spirit, Mr. Matthew Arnold was so fond of, plays round the consciousness of judges and legislators no less than of poets and thinkers.

The changes made by statute will hereafter be considered in some detail.

As to the new temper and disposition I have referred to, I do not hesitate to attribute it to the thrice-blessed abolition of affidavit evidence on the trial of actions in the Chancery division of the High Court of Justice.

The old Court of Chancery had many merits, great and striking merits, but it remained for generation after generation an entire stranger to flesh and blood. The " Man from Shropshire," poor Miss Flyte, and the rest were regarded as mad, and were hustled or wheedled out of court by the ushers and forgotten as quickly as possible. Chancery suits, above all things, required an unruffled atmosphere, and from year's end to year's end, the real live suitor, whose pocket kept the whole thing going, gave no hint of his actual existence. If he were ruined, as he too often was, it was done out of sight of judge and counsel. The only person who was ever called upon to witness his grief and dismay was the country solicitor.

I am just of sufficient standing at the bar to remember, as a student, the flutter of excitement occasioned in the court of a vice-chancellor when, on the hearing of some petition for payment out of funds in court, two or three married ladies would, one by one, be summoned to the bench to hold a whispered colloquy with the judge, who, as its result, usually asserted that the lady had consented to allow her husband to receive her share. To introduce these ladies to the judge, to tell him their names, and the precise amount of their respective shares, was a piece of business generally supposed to put a heavy tax upon the readiness and

resource of a Chancery junior, and it was
at all events his nearest approach to the
flutter of *nisi prius*, or the excitement
of cross-examination.

In this atmosphere it was possible to
decree much injustice without becoming
painfully aware of it. *Something* was,
with the utmost pains and acumen,
evolved from a mass of carefully settled
affidavits, which *something* usually repre-
sented nothing that had ever actually
taken place anywhere, and to that *something* so evolved all sorts of direful
consequences fraught with disaster to
living human beings, were neatly pinned
by trained intellects. An order was made
accordingly and further consideration
adjourned.

Now it is all different. The real Trustee,
for example, goes into the box—some
farmer, it may be, who from a sense of
cronyship has consented to act as a Trustee
under the will of a neighbour with whom

on market days he has often had a friendly
glass.   There he stands, ignorant for certain, pigheaded very likely, quarrelsome
possibly, but honest, palpably honest and
perspiring.   He is charged with losses
occasioned by his disregard of the strict
language of a will he never understood,
or for not having properly controlled the
actions of his co-trustee, the principal
attorney of his market town.

It may be necessary to ruin such a
man, to sell his horses and his cows, his
gig and his carts, and to drive him from
his old home, but it cannot be done without a qualm.   Hence has come about that
new spirit and temper to which I have
ventured to refer at too great length.

The present time is therefore a good
one to survey the subject and to consider,
first, the *Duties* and then the *Liabilities*
of Trustees.

We begin with *Duties*, for until there
has been a breach of duty there can be

no breach of trust and therefore no liability. The case of a Trustee deceived
by a cleverly-contrived forgery is an exception to this general rule and will be
considered in its place.

No breach of duty—no breach of trust.
A trust estate may be utterly lost, but
unless it was so in consequence of a
breach of duty, the Trustee walks away
scatheless.

What then are the duties of a Trustee?

The duties placed by me in the fore-
front have not usually such prominence
given them by the text-writers, nor is
this surprising, for the object of text-
writers is not so much hortatory as ex-
planatory. They are more concerned
with expounding the law than with es-
tablishing rules of conduct. But my aim
is severely practical, and I begin therefore
by asserting that the first duty of a
Trustee *is to make himself acquainted
with the terms of his trust.*

For this purpose he should insist from the first moment upon being provided (of course at the expense of the estate) with a full copy of the will or deed under which he is about to act, and by the terms of which he will thenceforth be held bound, and also with an epitome for readier reference of its chief provisions and powers.

For a layman the epitome is at least as important as the full copy, for though lawyers' jargon is often most absurdly abused, and, as compared with the jargon of doctors, scientific men, patent agents, stockbrokers, and theologians, is "the well of English pure and undefiled," still, as a matter of fact laymen do find it hard to keep their attention fixed whilst they are perusing a legal document set out at length, particularly if it is not divided (as there is no reason it should not be) into paragraphs.

Having obtained at the expense of the

estate this full copy and epitome, it is
the first duty of a Trustee so to read
them as to acquire a real knowledge of
the trust he has accepted. In ninety-
nine cases out of a hundred the trusts
will present no difficulty of comprehen-
sion to a man of ordinary education, and
a Trustee who has once fairly compre-
hended his trust, sets out on his voyage
with every prospect of making a pros-
perous trip.

But at the risk of pleonasm, I push the
matter further home. Not only must the
Trustee acquire this knowledge, *but he must
never forget it.* This is his Second Duty.

How often does it happen that the
newly-fledged Trustee, provided though
he may have been, either in consequence
of his own prudence or by the zeal of a
solicitor (not unmindful of costs), with
both a copy and an epitome of the will
or deed under which he acts, forthwith
and after but a hasty perusal, proceeds

to bury these documents at the very
bottom of a tin box, which is shoved
away in some rarely visited corner and
locked with a key not always forth-
coming. There they remain for years,
unconsulted and unthought of until, it
may be, complaint is made, and an action
threatened for a breach of trust.

The wise Trustee keeps these inform-
ing documents in the same drawer as his
cheque-book, and thus secures himself
from forgetting their existence; whilst
not infrequently, in those idle moments
which will occur in the life of the busiest
man, he refreshes his memory by glancing
over their contents.

I should not blame, but applaud the
man, who, being a Trustee under
numerous wills or deeds, had the
various Investment Clauses copied,
framed, and hung over his wash-hand-
stand basin, as hard reading men in my
time at Cambridge used to do with their

Paley sheets.   But if he takes this step
it must be at his own expense.

An enormous number of breaches of
trust are occasioned either by ignorance
or by forgetfulness of the actual contents
of the documents creating the trust.

Simple as duties one and two may
seem to be, and indeed are, their obser-
vance would prevent a large proportion
of the breaches of trust usually committed by honest Trustees.

The *third* duty of a Trustee is *to
adhere to the terms of his trust in all
things great and small, important, and
seemingly unimportant.*   This is his very
plainest duty ; no Trustee would ever
deny it, or pretend to be ignorant of it,
yet it is his hardest, unless from the very
beginning he makes up his mind to it,
and then it is as easy as eating bread
and butter.

The position of a Trustee tempted to
commit a breach of trust by the impor-

tunity of widows or the necessities of
orphans is not so very heartrending—if
only he recognises from the first what
he ought to recognise, namely, that he
has no right to make a new will for a
dead man or to depart from the contents
of duly executed deeds. *Non possumus*
is the one and the only answer for
badgered Trustees to give when pressed
to sell out London and North Western
stock and to purchase shares in South
African Gold Mines. Never argue or
reply to arguments, but barricade yourself behind your will or your deed and
whilst profoundly regretting your in-
ability to oblige, refuse to budge a foot.

The storm will eventually blow over, it
may for a few days rain black-edged
envelopes on your table, full of domestic
details of increased expenditure—now
Jack is at school, and Jane has to have a
resident governess—but *non possumus*
will carry you through, and after a while

there will be once more peace in your Israel.

To behave like this is not to be cantankerous but to be honest, not to be pigheaded but to be wise. Of course, if the case is so urgent as really to excite your genuine compassion, there is nothing in the rules either of law or of equity to prevent a Trustee *out of his own proper moneys* providing for the necessity of his beneficiaries, and if he does so he may possibly win their gratitude, but the ordinary way of being open-handed with other people's money seldom gathers any harvest save discontent, dispute, and litigation.

Now had my audience been composed of laymen I should be sorely tempted to bring my whole course of lectures to an abrupt but I hope not wholly ineffective conclusion. The three duties I have stated, acquaintance, remembrance, obedience, are in this matter the law and prophets, for no doubt, whenever a Trustee is confronted with an actual difficulty, or is threatened with litigation, he has but one course open to him—to consult his solicitor and to do what he is told.

But addressing as I do lawyers, I must abandon generalities and descend to details. I do so with some genuine reluctance, for the moment we come to consider cases and even statutes, we are apt to lose sight of those simple elementary duties, which none the less lie at the root of the matter. The native hue of our resolution never to commit a breach of trust becomes "sicklied o'er with the pale cast of thought" as we study nice distinctions between what is and what is not a breach of trust.

But bidding a final farewell to primitive truth. I approach the *fourth* duty of a Trustee.

The fourth duty of a Trustee is *to take*

as much care of the trust property as being a prudent man of business he is accustomed to take of his own.[1]

Lord Northington indeed, who was a very strong man and an able though somewhat hastily got up lawyer, electrified Lincoln's Inn more than a hundred years ago by this *obiter dictum*. "No man can require or with reason expect that a Trustee should manage another's property with the same care and discretion as he would his own," but, however shrewd this remark may be as an apothegm or criticism of life, it is bad law, and it is never cited save for the purpose of receiving censure.

[1] 'The duty of a Trustee is not to take such 'care only as a prudent man would take if he had 'only himself to consider; the duty rather is to 'take such care as an ordinary prudent man would 'take if he were minded to make an investment 'for the benefit of other people for whom he felt 'morally bound to provide,' *per* Lindley, L.J., Whiteley and Learoyd, 33 Chy. Div. 355.

" A Trustee" says Mr. Lewin, after shuddering at the frank audacity of Lord Northington, " is called upon to exert precisely the same care and solicitude on behalf of his *cestui que trust* as he would do for himself, but a greater measure than this a Court of Equity does not exact."

With great deference to Mr. Lewin this is wrong, not as wrong as Lord Northington, but still wrong. It would be no answer for a Trustee to say that he had bestowed the same degree of care and solicitude upon trust matters as he was accustomed to bestow upon his own, unless he could also go on and show that in his own affairs he acted as a prudent man of business of the day is supposed to be accustomed to act.

Therefore in considering this fourth duty we have to keep in our minds, and if we are Trustees observe in our conduct, rules of business, maxims of behaviour. How does a prudent, reasonably timid,

and justly distrustful man anxious to
avoid loss transact his own business? It
is far easier to ask this question than to
answer it.

The bulk of business in this country is
carried on carelessly. A distinguished
judge has told me that sitting in the
Court of Appeal he once had to listen to
a learned brother denouncing from the
bench as "grossly negligent," a course of
conduct habitually pursued by the distinguished judge himself in transacting
affairs for himself of a similar kind.

The truth is that in England business
is conducted on the principle that most
men are honest, and the larger a man's
transactions are, and the higher the
character of his usual associates in business, the less mindful he is apt to become
of rules of conduct which are observed
by men of scantier fortune or less exalted
character. A busy man in a large way of
business prefers to run the risk of making

a few bad debts, and having to put up in consequence with occasional loss than perpetually to hamper and pester himself with tiresome precautions. He is his own master, and prefers to do business in his own way, and at his own risk. But a Trustee is not entitled thus to endanger his trust estate—he must run no unnecessary or unusual risk.

But the question, How does a prudent man of business behave who is not anxious to save himself the trouble of proper precautions? is one of difficulty, and to some extent, as habits and customs of business alter and grow, one which may be answered differently at different times. For example—take the case of transmitting trust moneys. The now legalised custom of crossed cheques enables such moneys to be transmitted without risk in a manner which would formerly have been impossible.

If a Trustee were honest and prudent, and did all the work of the trust himself, no losses except unavoidable losses would ever occur to the estate, but this is what has become out of the question.

Nobody who has anything else to do could administer the smallest estate without employing an agent or agents. and if the estate includes lands to sell and stocks or shares to convert, unless the Trustee were both an auctioneer and a stockbroker employ agents he must, and if you employ agents you must trust agents within the scope of their proper authority. The solicitor must have the deeds in order that he may prepare abstracts of title or particulars and conditions of sale.[1] The auctioneer must be

[1] Trustees should not permit deeds to remain in their solicitors' custody for a longer period than is necessary. Whilst dealings with the estate are continuous, the deeds relating to that estate may properly be left with the solicitors. But as soon as that necessity ceases the Trustees should regain possession of the deeds.

allowed to receive the purchaser's deposits. The stockbroker must be supplied with the scrip, and allowed to complete the purchase or sale. The bankers must be allowed to receive the estate when converted into cash, and pending reinvestment or distribution. All these acts involve parting with the custody of the trust estate, or parts of it, and if the solicitor or the auctioneer, or the stockbroker play you false, or if the bank breaks, a loss ensues for which the Trustee will or will not be held responsible according to whether the confidence he has placed in those agents was or was not warranted by the ordinary course of business as conducted by prudent men.

There is nothing new in this law, for in the celebrated case of *Ex parte Belchier*, Ambler, page 218, it was held by that great judge, Lord Hardwicke, that Trustees are not bound personally to transact such business connected with,

or arising out of, the proper duties of
their trust, as according to the usual
mode of conducting business of a like
nature, persons acting with reasonable
care and prudence on their own account
would ordinarily conduct through mercantile agents, and that when, according
to the usual and regular course of such
business, moneys receivable and payable
ought to pass through the hands of such
mercantile agents, that course may
properly be followed by Trustees, though
the moneys are trust moneys, and that if
under such circumstances, and without
any special misconduct or default on the
part of the Trustees a loss takes place
through any default or neglect of the
agent employed, the Trustees are not
liable to make good such loss. The 24th
Section of the Trustee Act of 1893
embodies this law, and provides that a
Trustee shall not be answerable for the
acts, receipts, neglects, or defaults. of any

banker, broker, or other person with whom any trust moneys or securities may be deposited, unless the same happen through his own wilful default.

The question in each case, therefore, always must be whether a Trustee has, or has not, throughout the transaction which has resulted in loss, followed the usual and regular course of business adopted by prudent men in transactions of a similar nature.

In the now well-known case of *Speight* v. *Gaunt*, which was ultimately decided by the House of Lords in 1883, and is reported in 9 App. Cas., p. 1, the law expounded by Lord Hardwicke in the middle of the last century, was adapted and confirmed, and, as it were, carried down to date by Lords Selborne, Blackburn, and Watson.

In that case, a broker employed by a Trustee to buy securities of a Municipal Corporation, authorised by the trust,

gave the Trustee a bought note which
purported to be subject to the rules of
the London Stock Exchange, and obtained
the purchase-money from the Trustee
upon the representation that it was payable the next day, which was the next
account day on the London Exchange.
The broker never procured the securities,
but appropriated the money to his own
use, and finally became insolvent. Some
of the securities were, as a matter of fact,
procurable only from the Corporation
direct, and were not purchaseable in the
market, and there was some evidence
that the form of the bought note might
have suggested to an expert that the
loans were to be direct to the Corporation, but there was nothing, as the House
of Lords held, on the facts calculated to
excite suspicion in the mind of the
Trustee, or of an ordinary prudent man
of business, and it was accordingly held
that the Trustee was not liable to the

cestui que trust for the loss of the trust funds.

Unhappily, human affairs have grown too complicated to admit of the preparation of rules of conduct for prudent men, which should be so framed as to cover all the particular transactions Trustees are called upon to conduct; but I have often wondered we are as ill-supplied as we are with such manuals. *The Complete Tradesman* of Daniel De Foe, though not free from that irony which seldom forsook its author, is a kind of book which has been too scantily reproduced in other branches of business.

"Trustees whose duty it may become to select a broker, may advantageously read the case of *Robinson* v. *Harkin*, 1896, 2 Chy. 425."

II

In my first Lecture. after some prefatory observations, I expounded to the best of my ability four of the most important duties of a Trustee. Do not allow the first three to be obliterated from your minds, namely. acquaintance with, remembrance of, and obedience to. the terms of the trust; for were these duties observed. rare indeed would be the occasions when Trustees should be required to make good, out of their own pockets. losses to their trust estate.

The fourth duty of a Trustee :— namely, to take as much care of the trust property as, being a prudent man

of business, he is accustomed to take
of his own, was explained in connection with the early case of *re Belchier*,
in *Ambler's Reports* (a decision of
that great judge, Lord Hardwicke, all of
whose reported judgments you will do
well to read, for well do they deserve the
praise that has been lavished upon them
as " prodigies of learning and industry "),
and with the recent case of *Speight* v.
Gaunt in the House of Lords.

I hope those of you who are seriously
minded to obtain benefit from this course
of Lectures have already read for yourselves both these cases in their proper
places.   It would be easy for me to fill
up my hour by reading long extracts
from the Reports, but as no such labour
on my part would save you the trouble,
if you wish really to become acquainted
with the law, of studying the Reports
for yourselves, I prefer, though it is a
great deal more trouble, to express as

much as possible in my own way and
in my own language what I take to be
the law. and to give you the references
that will enable you to verify or correct
my impressions.

The fifth duty of a Trustee *is in all
investments to observe to the letter the
provisions of the trust-deed, or will, and
in the case of investment on mortgage
of real or leasehold estate, the requirements of Parliament.*

This subject of investments naturally
stands out very prominently amongst the
duties and liabilities of Trustees, for (so
some of my friends inform me) it is
very difficult to know how to invest
money.

But a Trustee is really in some respects
in a more advantageous position than a
private owner, because he has his
deed, or will to fall back upon. By
that alone is he judged—keeping within
the scope of his trust so long as he is

honest and does not deliberately inflict
loss upon the estate, he runs no risk
whatever.

Our first duty then is to consider the
investment clauses usually to be found
in modern wills and deeds. They may
be divided into two classes—wide clauses,
allowing a great range of investment,
and narrow clauses, greatly restricting
investment. For examples of wide
clauses of investment, I will refer you to
pages 68 and 70 of Mr. Wolstenholme's
Forms and Precedents, and to Key
and Elphinstone's *Precedents*, Vol. II.

Wide clauses, speaking generally,
include almost every class of rational
investment, and authorise a great many
investments which certainly do not
belong to what on the Stock Exchange
are called " gilt-edged " securities. Narrow clauses vary according to the
opinions or prejudices of the testator or
settlor. I have drawn wills in which no

investment of the trust funds was
allowed. save in bank annuities. As a
rule investment clauses run upon very
similar lines. and since the Trustee Act,
1893, which by its first clause authorises
Trustees, *unless expressly forbidden by
the instrument creating the trust*, to
invest any trust funds in their hands in
any of the investments specified in the
clause, it may be said that in the
majority of cases Trustees have power to
make any of the investments mentioned
in that clause, though sometimes their
discretion is restricted by the terms of
the instrument creating the trust.

But you will not fail to notice from
the language of the Act itself, that it is
the instrument which in the first instance
governs the investment. There is no
restriction upon the power of testators
and settlors to frame investment clauses
for themselves. They may throw open
their clauses as wide as possible, or they

may close them as narrowly as they
choose.

Therefore, in considering the duty or
corresponding liability of a Trustee in
the matter of an investment, go first of
all to the instrument creating the trust,
and learn from it what may or may not
be done.

But for the purposes of my Lecture
I will assume that we have before us a
will or deed which authorises the Trustees
either in express terms or negatively by
not forbidding them, to invest the trust
funds in their own names in the securities
or any of them mentioned in the first
clause of the Act of 1893.

The first securities named in the Act
are *Parliamentary stocks or public funds
or Government securities of the United
Kingdom.* These may pass without
remark, being " gilt-edged " securities.
But about the second class of securities
authorised by the Act a good deal has to

be said. These are "*real or heritable securities in Great Britain or Ireland.*"

Now first observe this means by way of *mortgage* and not by way of *purchase.* Trustees are not, in the absence of express powers, authorised to *buy* land as an investment. though they may as mortgagees foreclose and so become the owners both · by law and in equity of real estate.

You will observe that the statute includes Scotland and Ireland. As an Imperial statute it could perhaps hardly do otherwise, but apart from the Act of 1893 a power in an English will or deed to invest on real securities includes only England and Wales, whilst the Scotch Statute corresponding to the Trustee Act 1893 does not authorise the investment of Scotch moneys in Ireland.

Many testators and settlors take pains to exclude Ireland from their investment clauses, and in doing so no doubt give themselves the pleasure of indulging in their political convictions, but I am not aware that there is any reason to suppose that mortgagees of Irish estates have of late years suffered proportionately any greater losses either of capital or interest than mortgagees of English estates. But anybody may well wish to keep out of the Irish Land Courts.

What is popularly called a *second mortgage* is not within either the Parliamentary section or the usual investment clause; and this for a very good reason. The subject matter of a second mortgage is not land but only a right by paying off a previous incumbrance to secure the position of a true mortgagee. It follows from this that a second mortgagee has not the custody of the title-deeds, which always are (or ought to be) in the possession of the first mortgagee.

What is called a contributory mort-

gage is also "taboo." A contributory
mortgage is a first mortgage rightly
enough, but as the moneys advanced by
the mortgagees have been produced by
various persons clubbing together their
resources and taking one security for the
total amount in the names of all the
borrowers, it has been held not to be
a proper investment for trust money " in
the name or names of the Trustees."
Webb v. *Jonas*, 39 Ch. Div. 660.

By virtue of the terms of the 5th
clause of the Trustee Act 1893, a Trustee
who is authorised to invest in real
securities unless expressly forbidden by
the instrument creating the trust may
invest on mortgage of leasehold property
held for an unexpired term of not less
than 200 years and not subject to a
reservation of rent greater than a shilling
a year, or to any right of redemption
except for nonpayment of rent.

Let us now consider the case of an

advance of trust money on a first mortgage in which the Trustees are alone interested, of freehold or copyhold estates or of leasehold estate coming within Section 5. How is such a transaction to be carried out?

We already know from our Fourth Duty that the Trustee must act with ordinary prudence—but happily now since the Act of 1893, direct guidance has been given us. Trustees are not left altogether to find out for themselves what are rules of prudence in such a transaction. Prior to the Act of 1893 there was well known in Lincoln's Inn what was called an "ordinary rule" to the effect that Trustees should not lend more than two-thirds of the value on freehold land and one-half on land and buildings used in trade, and certainly this was a rule which nowadays, at all events, does not err on the side of excessive prudence. See *Fry* v. *Tapson*, 28 Ch. Div. 268. It was also a rule of conduct that the Trustees should not lend except upon the report of some valuer who was independent of the borrower.

But now it is not necessary to consider the law prior to the new Act which, on this subject at all events, amounts to a code.

Section 8 of the Trustee Act, 1893, Sub.-sec. 1, reads as follows :—

" A Trustee lending money on the security of any property on which he can lawfully lend, shall not be chargeable with breach of trust *by reason only* of the proportion borne by the amount of the loan to the value of the property at the time when the loan was made, provided that it appears to the court that in making the loan the Trustee was acting upon a report as to the value of the property made by a person whom he reasonably believed to be an able, practical surveyor or valuer instructed and employed independently of any owner of the property, whether such surveyor or valuer carried on business in the locality where the property is situate or elsewhere, and that the amount of the loan does not exceed two equal third parts of the value of the property as stated in the report, and

that the loan was made under the advice of the
surveyor or valuer expressed in the report."

On this section *five* points may be
made. First, the property must be
within the trust—that is to say, it must
be property on which the Trustee can
lawfully lend, and therefore if by the deed
or will the Trustee can only lend on real
securities the property must belong to
that class. Second, there must be a
report of value by a practical surveyor
or valuer. Third, such surveyor or
valuer must be instructed and employed
independently of any owner of the
property. Fourth, the loan must not
exceed two-thirds of the value of the
property as stated in the report. Fifth,
the surveyor or valuer must expressly,
and in his report, advise the loan to be
made.

This section is a bulwark for the
Trustee. If he first satisfies himself that
the proposed security falls within the

terms of his trust, and then proceeds to
take the steps so clearly indicated and
pointed out to him by the section, he
will run no risk for having made the
investment.

But nothing can get rid of the obligation of a Trustee to consider for himself
the character and nature of the security
he proposes to take by way of mortgage,
although if he has the report of the
surveyor referred to in Section 8, he need
not concern himself with a question of
value.   For example :   A Trustee must
remember in considering a proposed security that a *trade* or *business* carried on
upon land, is not a real security within
the meaning of an Investment Clause, and
he must therefore distinguish, and require
the surveyor he employs to distinguish,
between the value of the land forming
the real security, and the value of any
trade or business carried on thereupon
considered as a going concern.   The lead-

ing case upon this subject is *Learoyd* v. *Whiteley*, decided by the House of Lords in the year 1887, and reported in 12 Appeal Cas., p. 727. In that case the mistake honestly made by the Trustees and by the surveyor they employed, was that neither they nor he distinguished between the value of the land forming the security and the value of a brick-making business carried on upon the land considered as a going concern. In reading this case, as you should do carefully, do not forget that it was decided before the Act of 1893, and as you read the report keep asking yourself this question—How would the present law, as established by the Act of 1893, have affected the decision?

The initial question, Is the proposed security within the trust? must always be for the Trustees, who, satisfied that it is, should also ask themselves these further questions. Is there anything special, or

unusual, or risky in the situation or character of the property ? If satisfied that
there is not, then the Trustees have only to
observe *to the letter* the requirements of
the statute, and if they do this they run
no further risk whatever for having
accepted the security, although it may
hereafter become their duty to realise it.

I will now consider the requirements in
a little more detail.

First the Report. This does not mean
that the Trustees are to pay the costs of
the report out of their estate. By no
means. In this country, and I expect in
every other, the borrower pays all. No
doubt an intending borrower, who believes
himself to be the owner of a very eligible
property, upon the security of which he
has no doubt he can obtain from a private
lender, who is not bound by statutory
requirements, the loan of which he stands
in need, is often unwilling to make himself liable to pay for a report by some

valuer he may not know, and who may
prove so unreasonable as not to put a
sufficiently high value upon the security
to justify Trustees in proceeding with the
transaction.   If the report is favourable,
the borrower will not usually object to
pay for it, but if in consequence of the
report the Trustees refuse to lend it is
hard upon the borrower to have to pay
for the very document which prevents him
getting the money he requires.

This objection is sometimes pressed
upon Trustees as a reason for departing
from the obligation imposed by statute
—but they are fools if they do.   Such a
report is a *sine quâ non*.   Trustees, be it
observed, need not lend on mortgage at
all unless they choose.   They have, as a
rule, a wide range of investment from
which to select.   If they do invest on
mortgage, which is always an anxious
transaction, they must pay regard to the
statute, unless by the terms of their trust

deed they are expressly relieved from the obligation of doing so.

The surveyor or valuer must be chosen by the Trustees themselves, and he must not be in any way acting for, or on behalf of, the borrower; or if there is more than one borrower, of any of them. There is never any difficulty in finding out the names of respectable and experienced surveyors, and, although the statute does not require they should carry on their business in the locality in which the property is situate, it is usually wisest to employ men who have knowledge of the district.

The surveyor or valuer employed ought to be distinctly told in writing that the moneys in question are trust moneys, and that his report is to be made, having regard to the provisions of Section 8 of the Trustee Act, 1893, and he must be required, at the end of his valuation, formally to advise the Trustees that they

would be safe in advancing two-thirds of
the amount of the valuation. The report
should be signed by the surveyor or valuer
in his individual name, and not in that of
any firm of which he may be a member.
It is just as well not to tell the surveyor
or valuer the amount of the proposed
loan.

Having obtained such a written report
the Trustees must of course act upon it, if
they act at all, and not lend a farthing
more than the two equal thirds of the
valuation.

Another consideration arises. Suppose
Trustees authorised to lend money on
mortgage have been properly advised by
an independent surveyor or valuer that
they may safely lend a specified sum of
money on the security of a particular
property, and that they have done so.
Years go by—the interest is duly paid, but
depreciation in value sets in, and continues
to increase, so that loss in realisation is

ultimately incurred.   Are the Trustees
liable for a breach of trust in not having
realised ? In other words, was it the duty
of the Trustees in the early days of the
depreciation to call in the mortgage, and
failing that to exercise their power of sale?

It is quite clear that Trustees are not
bound to realise a security the moment
there is a depreciation in its capital value.
Who is to know the precise moment when
depreciation begins, or who dare say when
it has reached its height ? Looking back
upon a series of years this may be done,
but at the time it is impossible. Nevertheless, apart from the Act of 1894, to
which I am just about to refer, there can
be no doubt that Trustees may in some
circumstances hold on too long and consequently be guilty of a breach of duty
in not having called in or realised their
security, even though at the time when
the investment was originally made it
was a good one.   But I do not think mere

non-realisation can ever be a breach of trust unless the facts as to depreciation have been clearly established to the Trustee's knowledge in such a manner as to make continued retention obviously improvident and reckless. And now see *In re Chapman*, in the Court of Appeal, July 7, 1896.

The Trustee Act of 1894 provides by its 4th Section, that a *Trustee shall not be liable for breach of trust by reason only of his having held an investment which has ceased to be an investment authorised by the instrument of trust or by the general law.* The precise significance of this clause has not yet been judicially determined, but it clearly governs such a case as the one I have just mentioned. Consequently *the mere non-realisation* of a security originally good, but which has depreciated in value, is no longer a breach of trust. This section has been held not to be retrospective, so if at the date of the

passing of the Act a breach of trust
by reason of non-realisation has already
been committed, the Trustees are not
relieved (per Kekewich J. *in re* Chapman,
1896, 1 Chy. 323).

I may in this place conveniently
mention the 9th section of the Act of
1893, which is as follows : -

"Where a Trustee improperly advances trust-
money on a mortgage security which would at the
time of the investment be a proper investment in
all respects for a smaller sum than is actually
advanced thereon, the security shall be deemed an
authorised investment for the smaller sum, and
the Trustee shall only be liable to make good the
sum advanced in excess thereof, with interest."

This enactment, which sufficiently
explains itself, is quite new law, and
is a rule of great convenience for
Trustees.

Returning to the 1st Section of the
Act of 1893, which enumerates the
investments Trustees are authorised to
make unless expressly forbidden by the

instrument creating the trust. There
is not much in this lengthy clause to
engage our attention, though the whole
list should be studied by Trustees and
their advisers. This observation may,
however, be made. By Sub-section (g):
Trustees may invest trust moneys in the
debenture or rent charge. or guaranteed
or preference stock of any railway
company in Great Britain or Ireland.
incorporated by special Act of Parliament, and having during each of the
ten years last past before the date of
investment, paid a dividend of not less
than £3 per cent per annum on its
ordinary stock ; and by Sub-section (o)
Trustees are authorised to invest trust
moneys in any stocks, funds, or securities
for the time being authorised for the
investment of cash under the control or
subject to the order of the High
Court.

The investment of cash under the

control or subject to the order of the
High Court, is regulated by Rule 17
of Order 22 of the Rules of the
Supreme Court, and by that rule as it
now stands moneys may be invested in
debentures, preference guaranteed, or
rent charge stocks of railways in Great
Britain or Ireland, having for ten years
next before the date of investment paid
a dividend on ordinary stock or shares.
By Sub-section (g) therefore investments
of a particular kind may only be made
when a dividend of £3 per cent. has
been paid on ordinary stock, but by
Sub-section (o), and so long as Rule 17
remains unaltered, trust moneys may
be invested in similar kinds of securities
which have paid any dividend on
ordinary stocks or shares.

Having regard to the possibility of
alteration in the rules of the Supreme
Court, Trustees making investments of
this kind will be well advised to observe

Sub-section (g) rather than to rely upon Sub-section (o).

In making any new investment, or in changing an old investment for a new one, Trustees should require the stock-broker they may employ to state *in writing* the precise character of the investment he is about to make on their behalf, for there are nowadays so many different kinds of stocks and shares and debentures that it is well to have the actual investment specified in precise language. Trustees should never invest in bonds or other securities payable to bearer. Apart from the great risks of robbery and fraud such an investment is not an investment *in their own names* within the meaning of the majority of investment clauses. Nice distinctions may be struck between investments "in their names or under their legal control" and "in their names alone." Trustees should give such distinctions a wide berth,

and invest the moneys for which they are
responsible in their own names and in
securities requiring formal signed trans-
fers by all their number.

The *sixth* duty of a Trustee is *to give
the persons beneficially interested in the
trust such information as to the state of
the trust funds and otherwise as they
may from time to time require, and to
furnish such persons with accounts.* This
is of course rudimentary law, yet I will
refer you to a case in the books, because
I think you should read it, as an example
of the enormous pains and care, cost and
cumbrousness of a Chancery suit in the
time of Lord Eldon. No one can have
any pretension to be considered a lawyer
who has not some acquaintance with the
old practice and methods. The case I
refer to occupies the first ninety pages of
the third volume of Mr. Swanston's Reports, and is the case of *Walker* v.
Symonds. In the report you will find

set out at great length a bill in Chancery,[1] a joint answer, some several answers, a trust deed, a judgment of Sir Thomas Plumer, the Master of the Rolls, a decree of Lord Eldon's reversing the Master of the Rolls and referring certain matters to a master for his report, the master's report, the proceedings before the Lord Chancellor on exceptions and for further directions, and then the judgment of the Lord Chancellor.

The bill was filed in 1802, and the final judgment of Lord Eldon was de-

---

[1] "I called on the solicitor whom I had employed in the suit lately commenced against me in Chancery; and here I first saw that foul monster a Chancery Bill. A scroll it was of forty-two pages in large folio to tell a story which needed not to have taken up forty lines! And stuffed with such stupid, senseless, improbable lies (many of them quite foreign to the question) as I believe would have cost the compiler his life in any heathen court either of Greece or Rome. And this is equity in a Christian country."—*John Wesley's Journal*, Nov. 1744.

livered at different times in April, May,
and June, 1818.   A careful perusal of
this case—and it is a very interesting
one—will give you considerable insight
into old Chancery proceedings and also
into the law of Trustees.

But for my present purpose I must be
content to quote the observations of Lord
Eldon on page 58.   He says :—" It is the
duty of Trustees to afford to their *cestui
que trust* accurate information of the disposition of the trust fund—all the information of which they are or ought to be in
possession."   And again on page 73 :
" He who, undertaking to give information, gives but half information, in the
doctrine of this court, conceals."

Therefore although my proposition
requires no authority, I am glad to give
that of Lord Eldon for it.   A Trustee
must never withhold information.   This
seems easy, but it is not, for very often
the demand for information comes to the

Trustees in a disagreeable and even
insulting form. There are still too many
solicitors who, such is their ignorance,
conceive they are best consulting the
interests of their clients by writing the
most offensive letters it is possible to
imagine, imputing motives and half hint-
ing at fraud. Either to put such letters
into the fire and forget all about them, or
to write a furious reply is the alternative
which too frequently presents itself to
the honest and justly indignant Trustee.
But if he is wise he will do neither one
nor the other, he will keep the letter and
send the information. In the interesting
case of *Low* v. *Bouverie*, 1891, 3 Ch. p. 99,
the Lord Justice Lindley says : " The duty
of a Trustee is properly to preserve the
trust fund, to pay the income of the
corpus to those who are entitled to them
respectively, and to give all his *cestui que
trust* on demand, information with respect
to the mode in which the trust fund has

been dealt with and where it is." The
Lord Justice then proceeds to point out
that it is no part of the duty of a Trustee
to tell his *cestui que trust* which of the
latter's incumbrancers have given notice
of their charges, or to assist his *cestui que
trust* in selling or mortgaging his beneficial interest and in squandering or
anticipating his fortune.

As for accounts, a Trustee must always
keep and be ready to produce his
accounts. He is entitled to professional
assistance except it may be in the very
smallest and simplest of trusts. This
strict course is too often neglected in
England. North of the Tweed the
proceedings and accounts of a trust are
kept with as much formality as those of
a well-managed limited company. The
agent or writer keeps a minute book, in
which is recorded all the meetings and
the resolutions of the Trustees. At
stated intervals accounts are prepared

and vouched and balance sheets struck
and preserved. If in Scotland they are
too punctilious, here in England we are
too lax.

A *cestui que trust* is entitled to inspect
the accounts at reasonable times and to
see the vouchers, but he is not entitled
to a copy of the accounts save at his own
expense.

III

THE *seventh* duty of a Trustee *is not to make one penny-piece of profit out of the trust business, unless he be a professional man specially authorised by the instrument creating the trust so to do.*

There is no rule of law more deeply rooted in our English system of Jurisprudence than this. It is a rule without an exception. It presses very hard upon the natural man whose instinct it always is to make a little money if he can, but it has been applied by the Courts of Equity fearlessly—not only to Trustees of the kind we are now speaking of, but to all persons who stand in a fiduciary relationship to others.

Nor is the present time one when either
Parliament or judges are likely to relax
the pressure of the rule in any single
respect. The habit of secret commissions
given and taken every day (so at least it
is confidently asserted) by persons in good
positions, who account themselves, and
are accounted, honest men, is one to be
scouted by courts of law. It is the plain
duty of legislators and judges to hand
down from one generation to another (so
far as they can) untarnished, and of full
authority, those principles of absolute
integrity to those who employ you, or on
whose behalf you profess to act, which
are not only compatible with prosperity,
but are essential to commercial greatness
and well-established success.

If the rule I speak of has such a wide
extension, it naturally applies in una-
bated force, and unrelaxed vigour, to
express Trustees.

I could easily enlarge upon this rule

by citing some of the very numerous cases where it has been applied; but these cases are in reality more interesting to the student of human nature than to the lawyer, for they are but a record of the failure of Trustees to make a little money out of their trust. The judgment of Lord Brougham in *Docker* v. *Somes*, 2 Mylne and Keen, page 655, is an excellent example of the elaborate eloquence of that distinguished man. But it does no more than express in ornate language the rule I have already stated.

"Wherever," says Lord Brougham, "a Trustee, or one standing in the relation of a Trustee, violates his duty and deals with the trust estate for his own behoof, the rule is that he shall account to the *cestui que* trust for all the gain which he has made. Thus, if trust money is laid out in buying and selling land, and a profit made by the transaction, that shall go not to the Trustee who has so applied the money, but to the *cestui que* trust whose money has been thus applied. In like manner (and cases of this kind are more numerous) where a Trustee or executor has used the fund

committed to his care in stock speculations,
though the loss, if any, must fall upon himself, yet
for every farthing of profit he may make he shall
be accountable to the trust estate. So if he lay
out the trust money in a commercial adventure,
as in buying or fitting out a vessel for a voyage,
or put it in the trade of another person, from
which he is to derive a certain stipulated profit,
although I will not say that this has been decided,
I hold it to be quite clear that he must account for
the profits received by the adventure or from the
concern."

But not only must Trustees not employ
their trust funds in speculations on their
own account, but they may not (unless
specially authorised so to do) make any
deductions from profits properly earned
by way of gift to themselves, or on account of the trouble they have expended,
or as a small reward for the benefits that
have accrued through their exertions to
their trust estate. A beneficiary, if of
full age and under no legal incapacity,
can no doubt agree with his Trustee to
give him something for the trouble he

has been put to in the matter of the trust, but such a transaction will be viewed with suspicion and dislike by the court; and unless it can be shown that the parties were really at arm's length, and that no pressure was put either actually, or of the kind which naturally flowed from the relationship between the parties and the state of the case, it would very probably be set aside at the instance of the *cestui que* trust if he repented of his bargain. See *Barrett* v. *Hartley*, 2 L.R. Eq., 789.

As an example of the severity of this rule, and the ruthless way it has been applied, I will refer to the case of a solicitor who is a Trustee under a will or deed which contains no power to charge for professional services. Such a solicitor-trustee is not entitled, nor is the firm of which he is a partner entitled, to retain profit costs incurred in an administration action to which the Trustee was *qua*

Trustee a defendant, nor is such a solicitor-trustee or his firm entitled to profit-
costs incurred in the preparation of leases
and agreements of portions of the trust
estate. He is of course entitled to actual
expenses he has been put to in the matter,
but not to profit costs.

The judgment of Lord Cranworth in
the well-known case of *Broughton* v.
Broughton, in 5 De G. M. and G., p. 160,
states the rule as follows :—

"The rule applicable to the subject has been
treated at the bar as if it were sufficiently enunci-
ated by saying that a Trustee shall not be able to
make a profit of his trust, but that is not stating
it so widely as it ought to be stated. The rule
really is that no one who has a duty to perform
shall place himself in a situation to have his
interests conflicting with that duty, and a case for
the application of the rule is that of a Trustee
himself doing acts which he might employ others
to perform, and taking payment in some way for
doing them. As the Trustee might make the payment to others, this court says he shall not make it
to himself, and it says the same in the case of

agents where they may employ others under them. The good sense of the rule is obvious because it is one of the duties of a Trustee to take care that no improper charges are made by persons employed for the estate. It has been often argued that a sufficient check is afforded by the power of taxing the charges, but the answer to this is that that check is not enough, and the creator of the trust has a right to have that and also the check of the Trustee. The result, therefore, is that no person in whom fiduciary duties are vested shall make a profit of them by employing himself, because in doing this he cannot perform one part of his trust, namely that of seeing that no improper charges are made."

In the more recent case of *In re Cor-sellis*, 34 Ch. Div., p. 675, the same view may be found expounded.

The rule of *Broughton* v. *Broughton*, and *in re Corsellis*, is a wise one, because the moment you allow exceptions to a rule of this sort you insensibly impair its authority, and the mind learns to dwell on the exceptions, and to strike fine distinctions, and thus the clear-cut significance of the rule itself becomes blurred and blunted.

One exception has been successfully foisted on the law in this very matter of profit costs. In 1850 Lord Cottenham was found in a melting mood, and he allowed a Trustee, who was a solicitor, to act for himself and a co-trustee, who was not a solicitor, in a Chancery Suit, relating to the trust, and to retain the profit-costs—if the costs of appearing for, and acting for the two, had not increased the expense—which naturally it would not do. This was in the case of *Cradock* v. *Piper*, 1 McN. and G., page 664. One can well understand how Lord Cottenham came to this decision which indeed is sensible enough, yet it has been a troublesome decision, and has established an anomaly in the practice. If you carefully read the decision of the judges in the Court of Appeal *in re Corsellis*, you will notice how tenderly anomalies are

treated by English judges. They soon
become like ancient monuments or tombs
in the Abbey, things too old to be
removed. For what after all was *Cradock*
v. *Piper*? No more than a rule in the
Taxing Master's Office since 1850. Nobody has allowed his conduct to be
affected by it; no solicitor has ever
accepted the office of Trustee on the faith
of it. It has in no way affected the title
to property, or the liberty of the subject,
or the freedom of contract. Still there it
is, and there it has been allowed to remain
out of respect to a tradition, the origin of
which is certain, and the date recent.
But it is fiercely restricted to proceedings
in Chancery, in cases where the solicitor-
trustee is co-defendant with trustees who
are not solicitors.

By special provision in the instrument
creating the trust, the Trustee being a professional man, may be allowed to make the
usual charges; and such a provision is now

usually inserted in carefully drawn documents. It runs as follows : "Any Trustee being a solicitor, or other person engaged in any profession or business, shall be entitled to be paid all usual professional charges for business transacted, and acts done by him, or any partner of his in connection with the trusts hereof including acts, which a Trustee, not being in any profession or business, could have done personally." In this connection it is well to remember that a solicitor or other professional Trustee or executor will not be entitled to the benefit of this provision if he is an attesting witness to the will—and this upon the ground that this right, conferred upon a Trustee to make professional charges, is a beneficial interest arising under the will, from claiming which, an attesting witness is precluded by the Wills Act, 1 Vict. Cap. 26, Sec. 15. See *in re* Pooley, 40 Ch. Div., page 1.

The *eighth* duty of a Trustee is a commonplace, as indeed most duties are. *It is to co-operate with the co-Trustee or Trustees in a reasonable and proper spirit, and to consult with them about all matters connected with the trust, and to retire on being requested so to do by all concerned.* A Trustee should never get into the habit of either leaving a co-Trustee out of account or allowing himself to be so left out. The English law does not recognise the distinction between an acting and a non-acting Trustee. As a matter of business, one Trustee must usually take the initiative, and the other or others be more or less lookers on, but they must be *informed* and *critical* lookers-on, else they neglect their duty. No step should be taken without the conscious approval of all the Trustees.

Here the formal spirit of the Scotch practice is in remarkable contrast to the happy-go-luckiness of the English. With

us private express Trustees rarely meet
in conclave, nor is it usual to preserve a
record of their decisions. The trust
business is transacted through the post,
at odd moments of time, and in scraps of
conversation, and yet in theory our
law is stricter than the Scotch law. The
Scotch law allows a majority of the
Trustees to override a minority and
recognises a quorum sufficient for the
transaction of any trust business. Our
law does not recognise a majority, and
we have no quorum. All the Trustees
must be like-minded, and unless the
unwilling Trustee is obviously corrupt he
cannot be compelled, save by administration of the trust estate by the court, to
give up his opinion in deference to that
of his brethren.

The duty of a Trustee to retire is
worded too strongly. It is not the *duty* of
a Trustee to retire even when called upon
so to do by all concerned. Unless guilty

of misconduct, mentally incapable, per-
manently resident abroad, or a bankrupt,
he is irremovable. Even the court will
not remove him. But it always creates
a very bad impression when a man insists
upon retaining an unpaid office against
the wishes of his beneficiaries who are prepared to nominate his successor. It argues
either corruption or cantankerousness,
and either disposition—the former legally,
the latter only morally—is a disqualifica-
tion for the office of a Trustee. It is
however necessary to add that a Trustee
should never retire if he knows that the
object of the beneficiaries in getting rid
of him is to fill the vacant place with
some one who they know will not refuse
his consent to a contemplated breach of
trust.

The *ninth and last* duty of a Trustee
is, *whenever any question of difficulty
arises in the administration or management of his trust estate to take the*

*opinion of the judge in chambers by way
of summons.*

Great revolutions are usually wrought
in silence, and such a revolution in our
Chancery practice was effected by what is
now called Order 55, Rules 3 to 13A, of
the rules of the Supreme Court.

You must all of you who intend to
practice the law in the Chancery Division
make yourselves intimately acquainted
with these rules and with the practice
which has grown up under them, which you
will find in what we call the "White"
book, namely the *Annual Practice* for
each year, edited by Mr. Thomas Snow.
These rules, or something more or less
like them, have now been in operation for
twenty years, and a practice has grown
up under them of enormous benefit to the
suitor and to the huge relief of Trustees.
The costs saved by these rules would
build a fleet of ironclads.

I am old enough to remember as a

student the old practice of the Court of
Chancery, and the evolution of a particular kind of Chancery suit. A case was in
the first instance laid before a Chancery
counsel, as to the true construction of a
will, a copy of which accompanied the
papers. An experienced counsel was
usually able in a few moments to
tell into which of the many well-
known pitfalls the unhappy testator
had fallen. Sometimes he had left it
uncertain when the gifts he fondly intended for his descendants vested—he
had employed the word "issue," did he
mean "children"?—when is the precise
period of distribution—or what the effect
of a gift over on death without issue!
Either one of these, or some one or more
of the half hundred other teasing questions so apt to arise on every ill-drawn
will, was, or were, usually detected in a
more or less violent form. That was the
first step in a Chancery suit. The second

was for the counsel to write an opinion in which he cited one or two of the cases with which the courts were only too familiar, *Hill v. Chapman, Leake v. Robinson, King v. Isaacson, Leeming v. Sheratt,* &c., &c., and to conclude by saying it was impossible for the executors and Trustees to take upon themselves the responsibility of administering the estate under such a will except under the direction of the court. Then the papers left counsel's chambers to return in a few days with instructions to draw a bill of complaint. These would be handed over to a pupil, who would prepare the Bill according to instructions, probably making a beneficiary plaintiff, and the executors and Trustees defendants. In the first paragraph the will was set out omitting merely formal parts—the date of the death occupied the second paragraph—that of the probate the third; a few facts as to the state of the family of the deceased were spread

over the remaining paragraphs except the
last, which stated that doubts and diffi-
culties had arisen as to the true construction of the testator's will, and it had
become necessary to administer his estate
under the direction of this honourable
court. To this bill an answer was not
usually considered necessary, and the
cause would be set down for trial and
marked "short," and some Saturday
morning an order would be made directing
the usual accounts and inquiries as to
debts, funeral, and testamentary expenses, legacies, and incumbrances, and
so on. These accounts and inquiries were
taken, made, and answered by the chief
clerk, and involved numerous attendances
before him. In due course he would file
his certificate containing the result of the
accounts, and the facts elicited by his
inquiries—facts about which there was as
often as not no dispute at all, but all of
which had been proved strictly by affi-

davits and certificates of births, marriages, and deaths. The cause would then be ripe for hearing on further consideration.

In July the courts of the Vice-Chancellors and the Master of the Rolls used to be blocked with Further Considerations, and it rained briefs in Lincoln's Inn. The briefs consisted frequently simply of the pleadings, copy of the original decree, and of the will; the chief clerk's certificate, and draft minutes of the order it was proposed to take on further consideration. The cause would be called on, and it was then not infrequently discovered that having regard to the decided cases the original doubt or difficulty, whatever it was, which had given rise to all these costly proceedings, was really not capable of argument at all, and an order was made in a couple of minutes declaring the true construction of the will, and dividing the residue, after payment of costs, accordingly.

This waste of money, this squandering
of the scanty portions of orphans, is painful to contemplate even in the retrospect
of life.

All this is now over and done with.
Walk round the Chancery end of the
High Court on a Monday morning and
you will find only one judge, of first
instance, sitting in his robes trying witness actions; the other judges are all
sitting in chambers, that is in their courts,
but at the table, and not upon the bench,
up to their eyes in summonses, mostly
originating summonses, taken out under
the order referred to.   Leaders are con-
spicuous by their absence, and junior
counsel only are to be seen holding briefs
marked, it must be said, with unreason-
ably low fees.   It is hardly to exaggerate
to say that each one of these summonses
is a strangled Chancery suit.

Although I cannot here usefully go
through these rules or say anything likely

to save you the trouble of making yourselves personally acquainted with their
terms, I will set out that by them—

1. The Trustees under any deed or
instrument, or any of them, may take out
an Originating Summons in the chambers
of a judge of the Chancery Division for
the determination without an administration of the trust of any of the following
questions or matters :—

(*a*) Any question affecting the rights
or interests of the person claiming
to be amongst others a *cestui que
trust*.

(*b*) The furnishing of any particular
accounts by the Trustees, and the
vouching, when necessary, of such
accounts.

(*c*) The payment into Court of any
money in the hands of Trustees.

(*d*) Directing the Trustees to do or
abstain from doing any particular
act.

(e) The approval of any sale, purchase, compromise, or other transaction. and

(f) Determination of any question arising in the administration of the estate.

2. In like manner an order may be obtained in chambers for—

(a) The administration of the personal estate of a deceased man.

(b) The administration of his real estate, and

(c) The administration of any trust.

Rule 10 of Order 55 expressly declares that it shall not be obligatory on the court or a judge to pronounce or make a judgment or order, whether on summons or otherwise, for the administration of any trust or of the estate of any deceased person, if the questions between the parties can be properly determined without such judgment or order. And by Rule 10a—

Upon an application for administration
or execution of trusts by a creditor or
beneficiary under a will intestacy or deed
of trust, where no accounts or insufficient
accounts have been rendered, the court or
a judge may in addition to the powers
already existing—

    (*a*) Order that the application shall
stand over for a certain time, and
that the executors and administrators or Trustees, in the mean-
time shall render to the applicant
a proper statement of their
accounts, with an intimation that
if this is not done they may be
made to pay the costs of the proceedings.

    (*b*) When necessary to prevent pro-
ceedings by other creditors, or by
persons beneficially interested,
make the usual judgment or order
for administration, with a proviso
that no proceedings are to be taken

under such judgment or order without leave of the judge in person.

The young practitioner, nevertheless,
must be very careful as to his practice in
this matter of originating summons.   You
will have solicitors' clerks bursting into
your chambers demanding that you should
off-hand settle what they call "Origin-
ators," but you must keep your head cool
and remember that an originating summons is to all intents and purposes an
action, and that though no doubt the old
rules as to parties have been somewhat
relaxed, nevertheless the judge, sitting in
chambers though he be, will insist upon
proper parties appearing before him. and
will not determine important points in
their absence.   The rules of practice as to
parties will be found in the White Book I
have before referred to.

Next, it must be remembered that there
are certain remedies which cannot be
pursued by way of originating summons,

and especially remember that Trustees cannot be charged with a breach of trust by originating summons. See *Dowse* v. *Gorton* (1891), App. Cas. page 202.

Further, remember that the question about which you wish to obtain the opinion of the court, must actually have arisen—it not being the practice of the court to decide hypothetical questions which, in the course of events, may never actually arise.

IV.

WELL, Gentlemen, this concludes my brief summary of the *Duties* of Trustees.

I now approach the subject of their *Liabilities*. I have already said the liabilities of Trustees are to be measured by their duties. Unless there is a breach of duty there can be no breach of trust. Every plain dereliction of duty is a breach of trust and if a breach of trust results in pecuniary loss, the Trustee committing it is personally liable : *e.g.* to make an investment of a kind not authorised by the terms of the trust is to neglect duties Nos. I. II. and III.,

whilst to make an improvident investment on a mortgage security (mortgage
securities being authorised by the trust)
is to neglect duties IV. and V.

A Trustee cannot be made liable to
make good out of his own pocket any loss
which has accrued to the estate unless it
can be shown that such loss was occasioned by his doing what he ought not to
have done, or from his having omitted to
do what he ought to have done—he must
be guilty of sin either of commission or
omission.

Breaches of trust must therefore be
either *active* or *passive*.

Active breaches of trust rarely present
difficulty except in their proof. It is
unusual for an honest and ordinarily
careful Trustee to commit an active
breach of trust. To buy the trust property on his own account is an active
breach of trust. In no circumstances
must a Trustee do this, nor should he get

his wife to do it out of her separate estate
—not even though the sale be by public
auction and he be away from home at
the time.

To lend trust money on a second mortgage or other unauthorised security—to
mix trust funds with their own private
money — these are active breaches of
trust; and you can easily imagine others
besides the one I shall hereafter refer to
at some length—the continuing to carry
on a testator's business without being
authorised so to do by the terms of his
will.

Passive breaches of trust, *i.e.*, breaches
resulting from omissions, are more likely
to be committed by the unwary Trustee.

I will proceed to give a few examples
by way of illustration.

A. Non-conversion of the trust estate
directed to be converted.

Here it specially behoves the Trustee
to be on the look-out, for in times like

these in which we live, depreciation of property of every kind is at all events not unlikely to occur.

Under a will it is upon the executors rather than the Trustees that the duty of realisation of the estate is cast, but as after the payment of debts, funeral and testamentary expenses, and legacies, a will frequently declares trusts of the balance, and very frequently appoints the same persons Trustees who had been named as executors, it is difficult in this branch of the case to keep executors and Trustees quite distinct in one's mind.

Although there is no fixed rule of law on the subject, executors are allowed a year in which to manipulate their estate, and, if they admit assets, to pay the debts and pecuniary legacies. Executors ought to adhere to this rule, for if they do not and there is such a fall in the value of the testator's estate as makes it

impossible for them to pay the pecuniary
legatees in full, those gentlemen may say
to the executors—If you had sold within your year you would have realised
enough to pay us in full, and as you neglected so to do, you must make good the
difference out of your own pocket, and,
unless special circumstances can be shown,
the pecuniary legatees will not say this
in vain.

The motives for non-realisation are
usually pure. Stockbrokers advise that a
rise in a particular security largely held
by the testator is probable, and that if it
occurs not only will there be enough to
pay pecuniary legatees in full, but something will be left over for the residuary
legatees. But to take this advice is to
run risk. Executors have no right to
nurse the estate at the possible expense
of the pecuniary legatees for the possible
benefit of the residuary legatees. On
this point see *Buxton* v. *Buxton*, 1 My.

& C., page 80, and *Grayburn* v. *Clark-son*, 3 L.R. Ch. App., page 605.

In the case of Trustees properly so-called, there is no actual rule about a year, but by analogy this period should be kept in mind. See *Sculthorpe* v. *Tupper*, 13 L. R. Eq., 232, where a testator gave all the residue of his estate to four Trustees upon trust, to sell either immediately after his decease or so soon thereafter as the Trustees might see fit to do. Included in the testator's personal estate were shares in the Birmingham Banking Company, which was of high standing and repute at the testator's death. The Trustees retained these shares for two years and a quarter. The bank suspended payment. It was held that the Trustees, although they had acted in perfect good faith, and as they considered best, for the interests of the beneficiaries, were bound to have sold the bank shares within a reasonable time, which was one year from the testator's death and they were therefore liable to make good the loss.

Trustees very frequently, and indeed in all properly-drawn wills and settlements, have a discretion given to them as to when they should realise, and a power to postpone realisation. If they have such a discretionary power of postponement they may safely act as they may be advised; but they must never forget that it is their duty to realise whenever they think the right time has arrived, and that the power conferred upon them of postponement was not meant indefinitely to allow them to keep things as they are, but simply to enable them to realise to the best possible advantage and at the best possible moment. See *in re Northington*, 13 Ch. Div., 654. See also, and consider, *in re Crowther* (1895) 2 Ch., p. 56; and *in re Smith* (1896) 1 Ch., p. 171. In the latter case, Mr. Justice

North held that a power to postpone the
sale of all or any part of the residue
devised and bequeathed on trust to sell,
and particularly to sell the testator's
business of a pawnbroker with all con-
venient speed, did not give power to
carry on the business for an indefinite
time.

Whilst on this subject of the duty of
conversion, it would be a crime not to
refer to the famous case of *Howe* v.
Earl of Dartmouth, which you will
find reported and noted in the second
volume of White and Tudor's Leading
Cases. That case established the rule
that where property of a wasting or
perishable nature, such, for example, as
leaseholds, is given to persons in succession, such property must at once be
converted in such a way as to produce
capital bearing interest. In *Howe* v.
Earl of Dartmouth there was *no trust to
convert.* If there is a direction to con-

H

vert, there is no need of the rule of
Howe v. *Earl of Dartmouth*, for the will
containing the direction must be obeyed,
and disobedience is a breach of trust.
But the rule of *Howe* v. *Earl of Dartmouth* is this, that even when there is no
direction to convert, if the property is
of a wasting or perishable nature, and
the testator has, by the way in which he
has disposed of it, shown an intention
that different persons should enjoy it
one after the other, then conversion
must take place ; subject of course to
this, that the whole will or settlement
must be carefully read, to see whether or
no it contains any evidence of a contrary
intention.

A power in the will to retain any portions of the testator's property in the
same state in which it should be at his
decease takes the case entirely out of
Howe v. *Earl of Dartmouth*, because of
the power given to the Trustees to retain

the property *in specie*. See *Gray* v. *Siggers*, 15 Ch. Div., p. 74, and see *in re Thomas* (1891), 3 Ch. p. 482.

In my opinion, any person would be well advised if he refused to be a Trustee under a will which did not give the Trustees complete discretion as to when they should realise, and a power to postpone such realisation.

B. The second example I will give of a passive breach of trust is non-accumulation of the income for the benefit of the person ultimately entitled. See *in re Emmett*, 17 Ch. Div., 143.

c. A third example, and not an infrequent one, is neglect to enforce a covenant. The case of *Fenwick* v. *Greenwell*, 10 Beav., p. 412, is an example of this kind of breach of trust. By a marriage settlement it was covenanted and agreed that £5,000 consols, part of the intended wife's property, should be transferred to

Trustees upon certain trusts for the husband, wife and children. At the time of the settlement a sum of £4,946 2s. 8d. Three per cents. was standing in the name of the wife—but the Trustees took no steps to compel a transfer, and some eleven years after the marriage the husband and wife sold out the fund and the husband misapplied it, and in due course became bankrupt. The date of the settlement was 1806, and the bill was filled in 1846 by one of the children of the marriage to make the Trustees liable for the £5,000, which had been lost by their neglect to get it transferred into their names. The Master of the Rolls came to the conclusion that he could not see any sufficient reason why the Trustees should not have procured the transfer of the stock which belonged to the lady at the time of the marriage, and he observed: " It is with some reluctance that I have come to the conclusion that these Trustees if they had used due diligence might have recovered this sum to the extent of £4,946. It is a case of very great hardship. *It does not appear that these Trustees ever looked into the settlement,* but having contracted obligations by the execution of the deed they attempt to excuse themselves by saying that they were ignorant of the trust. This cannot avail them." A declaration was made that the Trustees were liable to make good the £4,946 2s. 8d. bank three per cent. annuities, and to pay the dividends which might have accrued thereon from the date of the husband's death, and also the plaintiff's costs of the suit.

D. The last example I will give of a passive breach of trust is the neglect to ask for, and obtain, title-deeds relating to the settled property.

The neglect of this duty is to fail to observe duty No. IV. Every prudent

man of business keeps in his own
possession or under his own exclusive
control the documents of title of his
property, whether deeds of conveyance
or of mortgage bonds, scrip or whatever
else they may be. To let other people
have access to these documents is to
invite fraud, and it may be to give to
third parties a superior equity to your
own. See *Lloyd's Banking Company* v.
Jones, 29 Ch. Div. 221, where a
husband having deposited with his
bankers certain title-deeds together with
a memorandum of deposit as a continuing
security to the bankers for any overdraft of his wife's current account, died
having bequeathed all his property to
his wife and appointed her his executrix.
After his death the deeds remained with
the bankers and the widow was allowed
to overdraw her account. Six months
after her husband's death the widow
married again. Prior to her re-marriage

she assigned the houses to which the title-deeds referred to her Trustee on trust for herself for life, and after her death in trust for an infant son of her first marriage. The Trustee made no inquiry about the title-deeds, and no notice of the settlement was given to the bankers, who obtained from the lady and her new husband a fresh memorandum of deposit, making the deeds a continuing security for any overdraft of the husband's current account. At the date of the wife's death the deeds were still with the bankers, and at that moment of time the husband's current account was in credit. Five years after the wife's death the Trustee made inquiries and discovered that the deeds which he had believed to be in the custody of the solicitor, who had prepared the settlement, were with the bankers. He then gave the bankers notice of the settlement and claimed the deeds, but it

was held that the omission of the Trustee
to inquire for the title-deeds was negligence of such a character as prevented
him from availing himself of the legal
estate, to give him priority over the
equitable charge of the bankers, and that
his *cestui que* trust stood in no better
position. It was also held that the
bankers were entitled to priority in
respect of the amount due to them on
their security at the time at which they
received notice of the settlement.

On this point of custody of title-deeds
it is not easy to say what the precise rule
is, if, as ought always to be the case, there
are several Trustees.

Supposing there are three Trustees
which of them is to have physical
custody of the deeds?

A box with three different locks
opened by three different keys one to
be kept by each of the three Trustees is
not a very practical idea, and then, after

all, where is the box to be kept? Such
a precaution as this is not considered in
accordance with the habits of mankind,
see *Cottam* v. *Eastern Counties Railway
Company*, 1 J. and H., 247. The case of
Mendes v. *Guedalla* in 2 J. and H. 259,
is well worth your study. It deals with
the case of stocks and securities payable
to bearer and which pass by delivery, and
upon which the interest is payable upon
coupons half yearly. Lord Hatherley,
whilst Vice-Chancellor, held that such
securities may without breach of trust
be deposited in a box kept at a banker's
on account of all the Trustees, one being
allowed to keep the key in order to
obtain coupons, the Vice-Chancellor ob-
serving that he · saw no irregularity in
one of the Trustees being left in possession of the key so long as the box was
deposited in the safe at the banker's.
The key must have been entrusted to
some person in order to get access half

yearly to the coupons, and to no person
could it be entrusted for that purpose
with greater propriety than to one of the
Trustees. Still my advice to Trustees
is, do not hold securities payable to
bearer at all, but purchase inscribed stock
in the names of all the Trustees. Why
should any man gratuitously run such
risks? Besides, as already observed,
bearer securities are not investments
"in the names" of the Trustees and
therefore are not authorised by the great
majority of investment clauses, and to hold
them is in most cases a breach of trust.

Passing away now from examples of
passive breaches of trust, we approach an
interesting and important point, the liability of one Trustee for the improper
acts or omissions of another.

Let me state the rule broadly and
affirmatively, and then consider by the
light of the cases, what qualifications it
may require.

A co-Trustee is not liable for the acts and defaults of his co-Trustee.

This has been the law for many a long day, and is at least as old as the time of Charles I.

The 24th Section of the Act of 1893 does but express in statutory form what was already, and had long been, the law when the Act was passed. Still you will do well to get its language into your heads.

"A Trustee shall, without prejudice to the provisions of the instrument, if any, creating the trust be chargeable only for moneys and securities actually received by him, notwithstanding his signing any receipt for the sake of conformity, and shall be answerable and accountable only for his own acts, receipts, neglects, or defaults, and not for those of any other Trustee nor for any banker, broker or other person with whom any trust moneys or securities may be deposited, nor for the insufficiency or deficiency of any securities, nor for any other loss unless the same happens through his own wilful default, and may reimburse himself or pay or discharge out of the trust premises all expenses incurred in or about the execution of his trusts or powers."

In the case of *Barnard* v. *Barnard*, 3 D. G. J. and S., 355, Lord Westbury said—

"Even if that which is assumed had been proved, namely that Boyle (a Trustee) struck out the crossing from the cheque and then received and employed the money, I should have refused to make the other Trustees liable for moneys which their co-Trustee got into his possession without their consent or knowledge, and by an act of dishonesty in fraudulently substituting a new crossing on the cheque to that affixed by the Trustees."

The case of *Cottam* v. *Eastern Counties Railway Company*, is a valuable case to study. There one of three Trustees was allowed to keep two railway debentures in his hands and receive the interest. He forged the signatures of his two co-Trustees to a deed purporting to be a transfer, and he delivered the debentures with the transfer to the purchasers, who acted throughout in perfect good faith.

The Railway Company registered the transfer and paid subsequent interest to the purchasers. The forger was convicted of his crime. The two Trustees then filed their bill praying that the purchaser might be decreed to deliver up the debentures, and that the Railway Company might be ordered to cancel the transfer—and it was held that they were entitled to the relief they sought. Had the decision been otherwise the Trustees would of course have been liable to their beneficiaries to make good the loss. On this head see the cases collected in the second volume of *White and Tudor's Leading Cases*, under the leading case of *Townley* v. *Sherborne*.

Unless therefore a breach of trust can be alleged and proved against a Trustee he cannot be made liable simply because a co-Trustee of his has committed default, but as I have already had occasion to point out, negligence is a breach of trust, and if it is by the negligence of one Trustee that another has been able to commit a fraud, the negligent Trustee is liable, not for the fraud of which he is wholly innocent, but for his negligence which permitted it.

I will give one example of this obvious application of the rule. In the case of *Trutch* v. *Lamprell*, 20 Beav., 116, two Trustees having properly sold out trust money, one of them handed the cheque for the proceeds to the other, who speedily applied it for purposes of his own. It was held that both Trustees were liable, and as the one who had misappropriated the money had disappeared, the effect of course was that the honest, but careless Trustee, had to replace the whole fund. The Master of the Rolls observed :

"This is one of those painful cases which unfortunately this court has constantly to deal with, where Trustees, innocent of any desire to benefit themselves, have failed to perform their duties, and the court is compelled to make them responsible. It is constantly argued by counsel, but the conclusion is as constantly rejected by the court, that a person who acts is not an active Trustee and is not liable because he has only acted for conformity's sake. It is a contradiction in terms to say that a Trustee who acts is not an active Trustee by taking upon himself the office of Trustee and acting. He becomes in that transaction at least an active Trustee, and is bound properly to perform all the duties appertaining to his office. I am of opinion that it is impossible for Holmes to contend with success that he was justified in paying over the cheque to his co-Trustee." See also *Robinson* v. *Harkin*, 1896, 2 Chy. 415.

I may here remark that there is no obligation upon the Trustee who is a defaulter to indemnify his innocent but negligent brother. See *Bahin* v. *Hughes*, 31, Ch. Div., page 390.

I pass on now to a difficult yet interesting branch of the law, namely, *Acquiescence.*

A beneficiary who has acquiesced in a breach of trust is debarred from complaining of it.

Acquiescence is a familiar defence to an action for breach of trust, but it is by no means a defence easy to establish at the trial.

What is acquiescence? It means assent. It denotes an assenting state of mind. A beneficiary who acquiesces is a beneficiary who has assented.

Acquiescence is less than concurrence, still less than instigation, it is merely assent.

But assent to what? Why—to a breach of trust! There can be no assent in the sense of acquiescence unless there is complete knowledge of all the circumstances which went to make up the breach of trust. A partial knowledge, good grounds for suspicion, are not sufficient foundation for the state of mind known to the law as acquiescence.

I do not know that you will find in any case any authoritative once-for-all definition of acquiescence in a breach of trust, but there is no great difficulty in extracting from the cases a good working knowledge of what is meant by acquiescence.

There must, I have already said, be knowledge of the breach of trust, and the knowledge must be positive and complete. It is not enough to say that the beneficiary was put upon inquiry, for a beneficiary cannot be put upon inquiry since he is not bound to do anything in self-protection.   It is the duty of his Trustee to protect him.

And the knowledge must be complete, for the beneficiary cannot be bound by acquiescence unless he has been fully informed of his rights, and of the material facts and circumstances of the case.

But knowledge by itself is not acquiescence ; you may know without assenting, and if you do not assent you do not acquiesce.

It is clear that a beneficiary is not bound the moment a past breach of trust comes to his knowledge to call the Trustee to account, or to take proceedings to make him liable. He may stand by for, at all events, a reasonable time, but if he waits too long the equitable doctrine of laches and stale demands may successfully be invoked against him.

This equitable doctrine of laches and stale demands must be carefully distinguished from the Statute of Limitations, which, as we shall see in the last Lecture, was for the first time applied to express trusts in the year 1888.

Leaving out of our minds for the moment the Statute of Limitations and considering only the equitable doctrine of laches and stale demands, you may ask, what is a reasonable time during which a beneficiary may stand by? Twenty years is an unreasonable time. A testator died in 1832—the bulk of his property was distributed in 1847, and on the 19th of February, 1872, a bill in Chancery was filed against the surviving Trustee, an old gentleman of eighty-one, for administration and for wilful default in respect of a principal sum of £815. The bill was dismissed, but without costs, as the Trustee had failed to preserve accounts and vouchers. *Payne* v. *Evens,* 18 L.R. Eq., 356.

But a delay of three years or four years will not prove fatal. See the case of *in re Cross,* 20 Ch. Div. 109, but in reading this case bear in mind the change in the law introduced by the Trustee Act of 1888, Section 8, and consider how *in re Cross* would have been decided had this Act been then in force.

It follows from what I have said that it is very difficult to prove mere acquiescence. It is a word constantly used, and the judicious pleader seldom fails to

plead it as a defence, but it is not very
frequently proved at the trial or inferred
by the judge.

Concurrence and *Instigation* are different matters. Few things are more common than for a beneficiary to concur in
and even—such is the desire of poor
mortals for an increase of their income—
to instigate breaches of trust.

First *Concurrence*.

If the beneficiary actively concur in
the breach of trust he at all events cannot call his Trustees to account. But as
the common run of English trusts are for
the benefit of a man or woman for life
and then to children, and as the beneficiary who concurs in or procures the
breach of trust is usually the life-tenant
anxious for a larger income—though his
mouth may be closed, those of his fledg-
lings, his callow brood, remain wide open,
and they can on their parents' death call
the Trustee to account who has foolishly

been tempted to try to increase the income which maintained these ingrates in the past.

However, the concurring beneficiary cannot complain.

But concurrence just as much as acquiescence implies complete knowledge. Nothing must be kept back by the Trustee, and the beneficiary must understand the exact position and must know that what is intended to be done and what he wishes to be done is a breach of trust.

Second *Instigation.* This needs no expansion.[1]

A beneficiary who concurs in or instigates to a breach of trust cannot complain of it. That is rudimentary law—elementary justice.

---

[1] " The ' legal mind ' chiefly consists in illustrating the obvious, explaining the self-evident, and expatiating on the common-place."—Mr. Disraeli writing to his father.

But it does not rest there. It has long
been law that a beneficiary, at whose
instance or request a breach of trust has
been committed, can be required to indemnify the Trustees to the extent to
which the beneficiary had received benefit
from the breach of trust, and this upon
the ground that the liability ought
primarily to fall upon the person who
procured the breach of trust, and who,
having got the benefit of it, ought not to
be allowed to victimise the Trustees by
treating them as scapegoats. The leading
case on this subject is *Raby v. Ridehalgh*
in 7 D.G. M. and G., page 104.

In that case personalty was bequeathed
upon trust for tenants for life with
executory trusts in remainder, but without directions as to investment. The
Trustees, at the instance of the tenants
for life, abandoned their original inten-
tention of investing in the funds, and
invested on mortgage, so as to obtain an

increased income. The securities proved
insufficient. The children filed their bill
charging the Trustees with breach of
trust, and seeking to make them liable
for the deficiency. It was found, as a
fact, that the tenants for life were anxious
to secure as large an income as they
could, and that it was at their instance or
request that the moneys were lent upon
mortgage. The Lord Justice Turner in
the course of his judgment observed :

"Now the *cestuis que* Trustent for life who
instigated the Trustees to commit the breach of
trust have derived from that breach of trust the
advantage of enjoying the increased income of the
fund not duly invested according to the trust, and
the consequence of that is that the *cestuis que*
Trustent in remainder have a right to have that
income refunded and made good by the *cestuis que*
Trustent for life. It is trust money received by them
under a breach of trust to which they were privy,
and the effect, I apprehend, must be that as the
loss which ought to fall on those who instigated the
breach of trust has been laid by the court upon the
Trustees, the Trustees are entitled to stand in the
place of the *cestuis que* Trustent in remainder for

the purpose of recovering from the *cestuis que Trustent* for life who instigated the breach of trust or their estates the benefit actually received by them in consequence of such breach of trust."

This is unquestioned law. but the facts must always be investigated very closely before it is applied in order to discover that the beneficiaries who are alleged to have concurred, were fully informed of the state of the case.   In *Sawyer* v. *Sawyer*, 28 Ch. Div. 598, Mr. Justice Chitty says :

" I hold that the law is that for the Trustees to be entitled to the order which they now ask against the estate of the tenant for life, it must be shown that the breach of trust was committed at the instance and request of the *cestuis que* trust.   I make no distinction between instance and request. but it must be shown clearly that the breach of trust was instigated by them and that they were acting and moving parties in it.   It strikes me as a novelty in law and a proposition not founded on principle to say that the person who merely consents is bound to do more than what he says he consents to do."

Accordingly in that case, the learned judge held that the beneficiary in question, who was a married woman, had not done anything to charge her separate estate. However, since *Raby* v. *Ridehalgh* and *Sawyer* v. *Sawyer* and other cases of a like character we have a statute to help us, namely, Section 45 of the Act of 1893, repealing Section 6 of the now partially repealed Act of 1888. Section 45 is as follows :—

" Where a Trustee commits a breach of trust at the instigation or request or with the consent in writing of a beneficiary, the High Court may, if it thinks fit and notwithstanding that the beneficiary may be a married woman entitled for her separate use and restrained from anticipation, make such order as to the court seems just for impounding all or any part of the interest of the beneficiary in the trust estate by way of indemnity to the Trustee or person claiming through him."

This section adopts the old law, but also extends it, for by the old law, the liability was only to the extent to which

a concurring beneficiary had benefited,
but here there is no such limitation. Be
it also observed that the *consent* of the
beneficiary must be in writing, but not
the *instigation* or *request.* See *Griffith
v. Hughes* (1892), 3 Ch., 105. There
used likewise to be a distinction between
the beneficiary who was himself a Trustee
and one who was not, but this distinction
has now ceased.

The statute, however, does not in any
way affect what I may call the metaphy-
sics of the question. In order to make a
beneficiary liable under the Act in respect, for example, of an improper investment, it must be shown not only that he
instigated, requested, or gave his written
consent to the investment, but that he
knew the facts which would make it a
breach of trust. Thus if a beneficiary
puts pressure upon his Trustees to invest
money on mortgage, full well knowing
that they were expressly forbidden by

the instrument creating the trust so to invest trust moneys, his interest in the trust estate may be impounded by way of indemnity. But if the trust deed authorised such an investment, and all he did was to put pressure upon his Trustees to make an investment of that character, and the Trustees proceeded so to do but made an improper investment on insufficient security, the beneficiary could not properly be said to have concurred in, or instigated, or consented in writing to a breach of trust. But if the facts of the security were brought to his notice, and it was pointed out to him that it was of insufficient value, and none the less he pressed for its acceptance—in that case he would fall within the section. See, and carefully consider, the important case of *in re Somerset* (1894), 1 Ch., page 231. As to married women restrained from anticipation instigating to a breach of trust (a thing they are quite capable of doing), Judges still feel some hesitation in impounding their interest by way of indemnity to the too complaisant Trustee. Were the Judge to be convinced that the Trustee had consented to commit the breach relying upon his being able to impound the interest of the married women he would probably refuse to make the order.

Since the first edition of these lectures an Act of Parliament has been passed (59, 60 Vic. C. 35) whereby Judges of the High Court, and in certain cases County Court Judges, are authorised to relieve Trustees either wholly or partly from personal liability for any breach of trust whenever committed if they have in the opinion of the Court *acted honestly and reasonably, and ought fairly to be excused for the breach of trust and for omitting to obtain the directions of the Court on the matter in which he committed such breach.*

Legislation of this character is becoming common, and if it be the mark of a good Parliament to extend the jurisdiction of the Judges, it is good legislation. Trustees will be foolish if they rely upon finding the Judges disposed to condone breaches of trust.

V

It will be, perhaps, useful to consider in this Lecture two of the most usual breaches of trust committed by honest Trustees. With the fate of dishonest Trustees we cannot be expected to concern ourselves; they may safely be left to the tender mercies of the law.

The breaches of trust most frequently committed by honest Trustees are—improper investments, and continuing to carry on a testator's business for the benefit of his family when they are not specially authorised so to do by the terms of his will.

I will take investments first, for although I have already said a good deal on this subject, I think I can usefully add a little more.

Investments are of *three* kinds: 1. They may belong to a class of security which is authorised by the instrument creating the trust; or (2), They may belong to a class of security which is unauthorised by that instrument; or (3), Though they may belong to an authorised class of security they may be improper, because insufficient, or for some other special reason.

Note, first, it is the instrument creating the trust which determines by its own language what class of investment may be made by the Trustee.

A Trustee cannot be blamed for making an investment authorised by the terms of his trust, unless it can be shown that the investment so made was not made in good faith—that is, with the honest desire to make a wise investment. For example,

if a Trustee were to be told by competent
persons that a particular security though
authorised by the terms of the instrument was a bad one, and that from facts
which had come to their knowledge it
would soon be worthless, and yet in the
face of such advice the Trustee persisted in
making that investment, he might be
held responsible for it.

Second—For a Trustee to make an investment outside the scope of his authority
as defined by the instrument is to commit
a breach of trust *ab initio,* and to incur
the penalties I have already explained to
you. If the investment turns out well, all
the profit, though it be £100 per cent. per
annum, belongs to the beneficiaries ; if it
turns out ill, the whole loss falls upon the
Trustee. If there is any uncertainty about
it, it rests with the beneficiaries and with
them alone to decide what they will do—
whether to take the security or to fall
upon the Trustee.

I do not think there ought now to be any great difficulty in determining in any given case what is an authorised investment ; but Trustees will do well to consider each investment separately as the occasion for it arises, and to satisfy themselves before making it that it is within the scope of their authority. If a Trustee first studies his investment clause, and then, if necessary, carefully considers the 1st Section of the Trustee Act of 1893, and requires from the stockbroker a written statement of the nature and character of the proposed investment, he will seldom, I think, be in a difficulty as to the scope of his authority.

A few technicalities he must remember, as, for example, that a second mortgage is not a real security, and that neither a contributory mortgage nor a Bearer security is an investment in his own name.

And if he chooses, being authorised so

to do, to lend trust money on mortgage of real security, he must slavishly regard the provisions of the 8th Section of the Act of 1893, all of which I have already gone through in detail.

The 9th section of the Act of 1893, already printed on p. 54, relates to investments of the third class, namely, those which though authorised by the trust are yet improper by reason of their insufficiency.

Another example of this third kind of investment, is when Trustees lend money on an authorised security but to one of themselves. This is an active breach of trust.

If we seek a reason for its being so, we may find it in the assumption of the law that the whole number of the Trustees bring to bear upon the question whether or not there is to be a particular loan, an impartial mind, and no man is to be taken to be an impartial judge of either his own

K

solvency or the real value of his property. But there is really no need to
seek a reason for so elementary a rule.
Trustees are appointed to preserve an
estate in order that its usufruct, and ultimately its capital value, may be applied
in a particular way, and if the guardians
of the estate become debtors to it, their
office can no longer be properly discharged. There may be three Trustees
and the loan may be but to one of them,
but the two lenders may die leaving the
borrower the sole Trustee.

I do not think I can usefully add more
on the subject of investments.

There is, perhaps, no more frequent
honest breach of trust than that which is
committed by executors and Trustees who
continue to carry on their testator's
business with his assets though not
authorised so to do.

A farmer dies leaving behind him
growing crops and a small stock, worth

hardly anything at an auction. His
widow is a handy woman accustomed to
the management of the farm, and two or
three of the elder children are useful
about the house. They all implore the
executors and Trustees not to break up
their old home, where living is cheap,
and occupation provided for the elder
children, and the younger ones are left
free to obtain a few brief years of education. The executors and Trustees, being
good-natured   men,   yield   to   these
entreaties,   postpone   realisation,   and
allow the few hundreds of ready money
that were in the bank, at the testator's
death, to be drawn upon for outgoings
connected with the business, which is
carried   on   after the usual fashion of
farmers in this country, without either
books or balance sheets.   One of the
younger daughters marries early, and goes
away to live in a neighbouring town with
her husband, who begins to think that he

would like to handle his wife's share of
his dead father-in-law's estate.   He con-
sults his cousin, a solicitor's clerk, who
pricks up his ears, gets a copy of the will,
and in due course writes a letter to the
Trustees asking for an account.   These
gentlemen consult their solicitor, who
advises them to wind the whole thing up,
which they proceed to do.   The result is
a net loss of a round sum of money for
every penny of which these Trustees are
personally liable, unless they can plead the
statute in manner hereafter appearing.

There is no getting out of it.   Pity is
not only akin to love as the poet tells us,
but to breaches of trust as well.   I know
it is impossible to block up the way to
men's hearts by legal maxims, but it is
the duty of a lawyer to make known
those maxims, and to explain the direful
consequences of disregarding them.

Executors and Trustees are not bound
the moment after a trader's death to put

an end to his trading concern, even though they are not authorised to carry it on. Their duty is to realise it as early as possible as a going concern—for were they not allowed this latitude they would have to put up the shutters on the day of the funeral, discharge the clerks and shopmen, and thus destroy the goodwill. They are allowed a reasonable time to wind up.

Mr. Justice North considered two years not an unreasonable time within which to dispose of a pawnbroker's business. *In re Smith* (1896), 1 Ch., 171.

But unless specially authorised by the will to carry on the business and employ the testator's assets or some portion of them in it, it is a breach of trust to carry it on save for the purpose of a speedy realisation.

What is the penalty? It is the old familiar one. Are there any profits? They belong to the beneficiaries who may pocket them without so much as a " thank you," and without allowing the Trustee a halfpenny for personal remuneration. Are there no profits, but only losses? Then those losses must be borne by the Trustees. This is the pleasing option which belongs to the beneficiaries, to take all the profits or to have all the losses made good.

But the case is sometimes a little complicated. Supposing the Trustees have carried on the business in conjunction with others, or have mixed up their own moneys in such a way as to make it difficult to determine what share of the profits can be properly allocated to the testator's assets—then, it may be, the beneficiaries will have to be content with having their capital returned to them with commercial interest, namely five per cent. per annum.

Partners who are not Trustees, but have shared profits derived from the use of trust property, are, if personally impli-

cated, under the same liability as if themselves Trustees.

Flockton v. *Bunning,* which is reported
in a note to the well-known case of *Vyse*
v. *Foster* in 8 Ch. App. 309, was a case
of this kind. There a testator had for
several years prior to his death carried on
business as a turpentine and tar distiller
in partnership with his brother, who pre-
deceased him. At the testator's death
the business was in course of being wound
up and the assets sold and realised. The
proceeds of sale were received by his
widow, who was sole executrix under his
will, by the terms of which she was entitled to half the income of his real and
personal estate for her life, and the whole
fund, subject to such life-interest in a
moiety, was to be held upon trust for
such of his children as should attain
twenty-one equally. The testator had
thirteen children. Mrs. Flockton thought
it would be a good thing for herself and

children to carry on the turpentine trade,
and accordingly she entered into a partnership arrangement with the defendant
Bunning and another man—she con-
tributing a portion of the capital. The
partnership arrangements were from time
to time altered and readjusted, and the
business was carried on until 1864, when
the partnership was determined and the
widow was under a power in the articles
bought out at a valuation. She shortly
afterwards became bankrupt. Six of the
thirteen children being still infants filed
their bill against the widow, her late
partners, and others, asking for an account
of the dealings of the partners with the
partnership assets since the last account,
and for inquiries and other relief. It was
clear on the documents that Mrs. Flockton's partners knew perfectly well that
she was working with trust funds. On
appeal Lord Hatherley, then Lord Justice,
said :—

" If, therefore, there ever can be a clear case fixing persons with the legal consequences of dealing with trust funds, this is that case. The case of embarking assets in a new trade is a much worse case than that of continuing the assets of a deceased partner in a trade, for there is generally great inconvenience in suddenly withdrawing them from the business, and the retaining them too long may be morally justifiable or at all events excusable. But I see no justification or excuse for taking what you know to be trust property and putting it into your business as part of your capital. What then are the consequences following from that act? The consequences, I apprehend, must be these: The partners make themselves co-owners of the fund and use it as co-partners. In such a state of things they are just in the same position as an original Trustee. Of the cases cited *Travis* v. *Milne*, 9 Hare 141, was more to the purpose than any other. The Vice-Chancellor there makes a distinction between a fund advanced by way of loan and a fund mixed up with the consequences and liabilities of trade. In the one case the firm are borrowing money, their liability as to which may be probably more restricted than their liability as to trust money which they appropriate as part of their capital. But in the case before us there was a clear appropriation of the trust fund by all the three partners. I cannot, therefore, feel any difficulty in saying that the case is one to which *Travers* v. *Milne* is applicable, and that it is brought to the ordinary case of Trustees employing a trust fund and being answerable for the use they make of it. The decree therefore is substantially right."

The decree thus affirmed declared that Mrs. Flockton and her late partners were bound to restore and make good to the plaintiffs such part of the assets of the testator as had been employed by the defendants in trade together with all profits made by such employment, or with interest at the rate of £5 per cent. per annum upon what had been so employed.

Having mentioned *Vyse* v. *Foster*, I will just say that in that case the court held that by the terms of the articles of partnership a deceased partner's share retained in the business was retained in such a way as to amount to a debt due from the partnership firm to the executors of the deceased partner, and that although the executors had unduly delayed the calling in of this debt, such delay did not entitle a beneficiary to share in the profits of the business, and this notwithstanding the fact that one of the executors was himself a partner in the firm.

I hope I have said enough to warn executors and Trustees of the danger of consenting to carry on any trade or business save for the purpose of speedy realisation unless they are expressly authorised by the will so to do.

But suppose they are authorised the consequences even then are disagreeable enough.

In the first place they become personally liable for debts, although only acting as executors or Trustees. See *Labouchere* v. *Tucker*, 11 Moore's Privy Council Cases, 198.

In the case of *in re Morgan, Pillgrem*

v. *Pillgrem*, 18 Ch. Div., page 93, Mr.
Justice Fry, as he then was, observed—

" It appears to me that the principles which
regulate questions of this sort are very clear. As
I understand them, where a Trustee or executor
carries on a business under the directions contained
in the will of the testator and in that character
contracts a debt, the debt is one for which an
action must be brought against the executor personally, and for which judgment must be obtained
de bonis propriis of the executor, and no action can
be successfully brought against the executor as
executor and no execution can be had *de bonis
testatoris* for this very simple reason that the debt
was not the debt of the testator."

The distinction must of course be borne
in mind in cases of this kind between
debts contracted in the business by the
testator himself whilst he was carrying it
on, and debts subsequently contracted by
the executors or Trustees who continue to
carry on the business after the testator's
death in pursuance of directions contained
in his will.   The creditors of the testator

himself have of course a right to be paid
out of his assets, and can take proceedings to render such assets available for
the payment of their debts. But the
subsequent creditors can only look to the
executor, and to the goods of the executor, and they have no original right to
be paid out of the testator's assets, nor
does it make any difference that the
executor has carried on the business in
his own name, or that the testator's
assets employed in it are ostensibly the
executor's own property. See *Dawson*
v. *Wood*, 3 Taunt, page 256, and other
cases cited in *in re Morgan*, 18 Ch.
Div., 99.

But though the executor or Trustee
carrying on a business pursuant to the
directions contained in the will, is personally liable for debts contracted in
so doing, he is entitled to indemnity
in respect thereof out of the estate of the
deceased. This is a claim or right which

he has as against all persons claiming
under the will.

This right to an indemnity will be
restricted to that specific portion of the
trust estate which the testator authorised
to be employed in the conduct of his
business.   If he authorised the whole of
his estate to be so employed, of course the
Trustee may look to that whole, but if, on
the other hand, he stated the specific
amount he wished to be so employed, the
Trustee can only look for his indemnity
to that specific amount.

On this right of the executors and
Trustees to an indemnity a further right
has been grafted by legal decision, namely
the right of the creditors of the trade to
stand in the place of the executor and
Trustee, and to claim the benefit of that
right so as to obtain payment of their
debts.   An excellent exposition of this
law will be found in the judgment of
the late Master of the Rolls, Sir George

Jessel, in the case of *in re Johnson Shearman* v. *Robinson*, 15 Ch. Div., 548. Sir George Jessel says on page 552 :

"I understand the doctrine to be this, that where a Trustee is authorised by a testator or by a settlor—for it makes no difference—to carry on a business with certain funds which he gives to the Trustee for that purpose, the creditor who trusts the executor has a right to say : 'I had the personal liability of the man I trusted and I have also a right to be put in his place against the assets ; that is, I have a right to the benefit of indemnity or lien which he has against the assets devoted to the purposes of the trade.' The first right is his general right by contract, because he trusted the Trustee or executor ; he has a personal right to sue him and to get judgment and make him a bankrupt. The second right is a mere corollary to these numerous cases in equity in which persons are allowed to follow trust assets. The trust assets having been devoted to carrying on the trade it would not be right that the *cestui que* trust should get the benefit of the trade without paying the liabilities, therefore the court says to him : 'You shall not set up a Trustee who may be a man of straw and make him a bankrupt to avoid the responsibility of the assets for carrying on the trade.' The court puts the creditor, so to speak, as I understand it, in the place of the Trustee."

In such cases it is a matter of necessity that there should be a special part of the estate appropriated to carry on the business. See *Strickland* v. *Symons*, 26 Ch. Div., 245, where by a marriage settlement a lunatic asylum was assigned to Trustees on trust at the request of the husband to sell, but the Trustees were to allow the husband to carry on the business of the asylum on certain terms. The husband became bankrupt, and thereupon the surviving Trustee of the settlement took possession of the asylum and carried on the business there until it was sold for a large sum of money. A tradesman had supplied the Trustees with goods for the use of the asylum. He brought his action claiming payment out of the trust funds of the settlement. But it was held that he had no right so to do, as no special part of the estate

had been appropriated for carrying on
the asylum. Lord Selborne stated in
his judgment that it was impossible to
compare the case with *ex parte Garland*
10 Vesey 110, and the case of *re Johnson*,
which is referred to, and the other
cases where there has been an express
direction by the testator to carry on a
business, and where he specially appropriated part of his property for that
purpose. And the Lord Chancellor
added :

"Those authorities proceed on this principle,
that where a particular part of a trust estate is
specifically dedicated to a particular purpose
which involves trade debts and liabilities, it is a
trust to use it for that particular purpose, and the
Trustee though personally liable for the debts
which he contracts in the course of the business,
has a right to be paid out of the specific assets
appropriated for that purpose, and the trade
creditors are not to be disappointed of payment so
far as the assets so appropriated are concerned."

I may add that creditors cannot be in

L

any better position than the executor or Trustee in whose shoes they seek to stand, and if therefore the Trustee is in default, the creditors are not entitled to have their debts paid out of the specific assets, unless and until the default is made good. See *in re Johnson* 15 Chy. D. 548.

An executor or Trustee who consents to carry on the testator's business, even when authorised so to do by his will, certainly exposes himself to greater liabilities than anybody ought to be expected to accept at the request of another. I must now leave the subject and pass on.

There are two familiar and ominous words often used in connection with Trustees which require explanation—they are, wilful default.

A Trustee is in wilful default who has been guilty of a passive breach of trust, that is to say, who has omitted to do

something which he ought as a Trustee
to have done.

There were two forms of calling a
Trustee to account in the old Court of
Chancery—one ran thus :—An account
of the principal money subject to the
trusts of the will or settlement received
by the defendants, the Trustees or
either of them, or by any person or
persons by their order, or for their use
as Trustees or Trustee. The other ran
thus :—An account of the principal money
subject to the trusts of the will or settlement as have been received by the
Trustees or either of them, or by any
person or persons by their order or for
their use, *or which might but for their
wilful default have been so received.*

Under the first or common decree or
order, a Trustee could not be made to
account for moneys he had not actually
received. For example : in *re Fryer* 3
K and J. 317, lands were devised

to three Trustees, upon trust for sale.
They were sold and the purchase money
paid to one of them who was a solicitor,
and who acted in the matter of the sale
as solicitor for himself and the other
Trustees. This solicitor retained the
money and lost it, and the suit was
commenced for the administration of
the testator's estate and the common
decree was made. When the cause came
on for further consideration, counsel for
the plaintiff sought to charge one of
the defendants with the money so
allowed to remain in the hands of the
solicitor. But the Vice-Chancellor held
that the Trustee who had not received
the money could not upon the common
decree by which the question of wilful
neglect and default was not put in issue,
be made liable for its loss. Had the
decree been in the second form he might
very likely have been found liable to
make good the loss on account of his

negligence in allowing his co-Trustee to retain the trust funds in his hands for longer than was reasonably necessary.

To obtain an order on the footing of wilful default, some one act of wilful default must be alleged and proved. This was Lord Eldon's rule. In order to obtain an inquiry as to wilful neglect and default against an executor or a Trustee, the plaintiff must allege and prove at least one act of wilful neglect or default. See observations of Lord Justice Knight Bruce in *Coape* v. *Carter* 2 D.G. M. and G. 298, and of the Vice-Chancellor Wood in *Sleight* v. *Lawson*, 2 K. and J. 292. Under the old practice some one instance of wilful default had to be proved at the hearing because no such inquiry could be added afterwards. At the present day the substance remains the same. If in the prosecution of inquiries under an ordinary decree, facts come out which if proved at the hearing would have enabled the plaintiff to obtain an inquiry as to wilful default, then such an inquiry will be added. But the rule still remains that an account on the footing of wilful neglect or default will not be granted unless it has been pleaded, and until evidence has been given of at least one instance of wilful default. See observations of Lord Justice Cotton in *re Youngs*, 30 Ch. Div., 431.

Mr. Justice Fry in *Barber* v. *Mackrell* 12 Ch. Div. 538, put the law thus :—

"Those cases" (as to wilful default) "appear to me to come to this, that where wilful default is not pleaded no order can be made on the footing of wilful default either at the hearing or at any subsequent time ; but that where wilful default has been alleged, and a case is made for it on the pleadings, an account on the footing of wilful default can be directed either at the hearing or trial of the action, or at any subsequent stage."

It is, however, the duty of the plaintiff to be ready to prove his allegation at the hearing, and if he is not ready the court will not, unless a strong case is made, postpone inquiry into the conduct of the Trustees. See *Smith* v. *Armitage*, 24 Ch. Div., 727.

I may here repeat that accounts on the footing of wilful default cannot be directed on an originating summons, even though the parties to be charged are plaintiffs submitting to an account.

Where a beneficiary's action is not confined to seeking relief in respect of a particular breach of trust, but seeks a general account of the trust estate on the footing of wilful neglect and default, all the Trustees and the personal representatives of such of them as may be dead are necessary parties to the suit— *Cappard* v. *Allen*, 2 D.G. J. and S., 173. This rule is still one which requires attention, though it has been more lately decided that in an action brought by *cestui que* trust against a sole surviving

Trustee for an account, and asking for a declaration that he had committed breaches of trust, the plaintiffs were not bound to make the representatives of a deceased Trustee parties—but this upon the ground that if the defendant required them he could get them added under the new rules.   See *in re* Harrison (1891), 2 Ch. 349.

As a rule of pleading, it must be remembered that in all cases in which the party pleading relies on any wilful default the particulars of it must be stated in the pleading.   See Order 19, Rule 6.

VI

I HAVE reserved as the main subject of my last Lecture, a great novelty introduced into the law of express trusts by the Trustee Act of 1888, the 8th Section of which still remains unrepealed.

By that section Statutes of Limitation may be pleaded by Trustees subject to certain exceptions which I will carefully consider in a minute or two.

The principle of *prescription* and *limitation of actions* is a principle of some antiquity in our law, and one which is to be found in the codes and systems of both eastern and western nations.

Our own Statutes of Limitation have been made the subject of great praise.

They have been called by eminent judges Statutes of Repose and Acts of Peace ; in these respects resembling the thirty-nine articles of our religious faith as by law established.

In my mind they are always associated with an eloquent passage in a speech delivered in the House of Commons in the year 1844 by a distinguished member of our profession, Mr. T. B. Macaulay. Speaking on the second reading of the Dissenters Chapels Bill he reminded the House that the principle of prescription was to be found all the world over, and said something like this—

"It is in every known part of the world, in every civilised age; it was familiar to the old tribunals of Athens, it formed part of the Roman jurisprudence, and was spread with the imperial power over the whole of Europe. It was recognised after the French Revolution, and when the code Napoleon was formed that very principle of pre-scription was not forgotten. We find it both in the east and the west ; it is recognised by tribunals beyond the Mississippi and in countries that had never heard of Justinian and had no translation of the Pandects. In all places we find it acknowledged as a sacred principle of legislation. In our own country we find it coëval with the beginning of our laws. It is found in the first of our statutes—it is close upon our great first Forest Charter; it is consecrated by successive Acts of Parliament; it is introduced into the Statute of Merton; it is found in the Statute of Westminster; and the principle only becomes more stringent as it is carried out by a succession of great legislators and statesmen down to our own time.

"Now, how is it possible to believe that the Barons whose seals are upon our Great Charter would have perfectly agreed with the great Jurists who framed the Code Napoleon with the most learned English Lawyers of the nineteenth century, and with the Pundits of the Benares unless there had been some strong and clear reason which necessarily led men of sense in every age and country to the same conclusion.

Lord Macaulay, it is well known, was very adverse to the republication of his speeches. However, an unscrupulous publisher relying upon the then state of the law on such subjects published

without the great orator's permission an
edition of his speeches both in Parliament
and out of it. This piracy was in its
turn pirated by the pirates of the United
States, where there was a great sale of
the volumes. In both the English and
the American edition, instead of the word
" Pundits of the Benares," there occur the
words "Pandects of the Benares." The
nonsense thus made of his rhetoric drove
Macaulay well-nigh distracted, and was
the main cause which induced him to see
through the press that authorised edition
of his speeches which certainly has
justly swelled his fame.[1]

In ancient times the principle of
limitation had naturally most application
to the recovery of real estate, and as
defined by Lord Coke " is a certain time

[1] It is interesting to compare Mr. Vizetelli's
" pirate " Edition with the orator's own corrected
Edition. Neither the one nor the other repro-
duces the speeches as actually delivered.

prescribed by statute within the which the demandant in an action must prove himself or some of his ancestors to be seized." Lord Coke proceeds: " In ancient times the limitation in a Writ of Right was from the time of Henry I. After that by the Statute of Merton the limitation was from the time of Henry II., and by the Statute of Westminster the limitation was from the time of Richard I." Subsequently a Statute of Henry VIII. reduced the time to sixty years next before the writ, but now the Statutes of Limitation, which are still numerous, begin with the well-known statutes of James I., which, however, as to real estate have been subsequently much modified.

To go into detail on this subject would be out of place, but I may just say that as the law now stands actions of debt and of account and so on, must be brought within six years next after the cause of such action and not after, and actions for the recovery of land must be brought within twelve years next after the time at which the right to bring such action shall have first accrued.

The admiration felt and expressed for Statutes of Limitation by common law judges and Lord Macaulay has never been so cordially expressed by the authorities in equity ; for though the Chancery judges have always been unwilling to give encouragement to the notion that there was of necessity anything morally wrong in a defendant relying upon a Statute of Limitation, still they were usually careful to point out that the defence was the creature of positive law and not therefore to be extended to cases not strictly within the enactment. See observations of Lord Cranworth in *Roddam* v. *Morley*, 1 D. G. and J., 23. About one thing the Chancery judges never allowed any doubt, and that was that express trusts were not within the statutes. The Lord

Justice Turner, a most eminent master of
equity, in *Obee* v. *Bishop*, 1 D. G. F. and
J., 137, said (in 1859) that it would be
most dangerous to hold that a demand
against the assets of a deceased Trustee
or personal representative in respect of a
breach of trust or misappropriation committed by him was barred at the expira-
tion of six years from his death. It will
be observed that the Lord Justice did not
strike the distinction between an honest
breach of trust and a dishonest one.

So recently as the Judicature Act of
1873, it was enacted by Section 25, sub-
Section 2, that no claim of a beneficiary
against his Trustee for any property
held on express trust or in respect
of any breach of such trust, should be
held to be barred by any Statute of
Limitation.

I have pointed out in a former Lecture
that the distinction must always be borne
in mind between the plea of the statute

and the equitable doctrine of laches or stale demands. Before the Act of 1888, a *cestui que* trust might be barred by the application of the equitable doctrine of laches or stale demands, but in the case of an express trust it would have been idle and ridiculous for a Trustee, or for the representatives of a deceased Trustee, to have pleaded in a Chancery suit the Statutes of Limitations, or any of them.

Then all of a sudden, like a bolt from the blue, came the Act of 1888.

This Act is an interesting example of how, in this country, those laws are made, which affect (far more than hotly-contested constitutional changes) the habits and liabilities of Her Majesty's liege subjects. It is, I believe, quite true to say, that democratically governed as we are alleged to be, the laws which most nearly affect us are never subjected to our review, nor is our opinion (speaking of the people generally) ever sought upon the subject.

I have been told, though I cannot
vouch for the truth of the story, that
the genesis of the Act of 1888 was something like this :

A Chancery practitioner, who was also
a Member of Parliament, happening to
meet the Chancellor of the day. an eminent common lawyer, remarked to him,
that it had sometimes struck the Chancery
practitioner, in the course of his practice,
as somewhat of a hardship that a Trustee, or the representative of a deceased
Trustee. was not allowed to plead the
Statute of Limitations as a defence to an
honest breach of trust. The eminent
Chancellor expressed great surprise at
hearing that this was the actual state of
the law, and suggested to the practitioner
that he would do well to draft a bill for
its alteration. This was done, and the
bill became law, as such bills are apt to
do without much notice or discussion ;
and so in a moment the well-considered

judgments and opinions of a long race of
eminent Chancery judges were contempt-
uously disregarded, and to the great and
wholly unexpected relief of Trustees
the Act of 1888 came upon the Statute
Book.

Turning now to Section 8, and reading
it, in the first instance, without the exceptions, it runs as follows :—

> "In any action or other proceeding against a
> Trustee or any person claiming through him, the
> following provisions shall apply :—
>
> "(a) All rights and privileges conferred by any
> Statute of Limitations shall be enjoyed in the like
> manner and to the like extent as they would have
> been enjoyed in such action or other proceeding
> if the Trustee or person claiming through him
> had not been a Trustee or person claiming through
> him."

An eminent judge of the Chancery
Division once threw a distressing doubt
upon the value of this sub-section, going
so far as to say that he could not discover
in it any meaning at all.   He pointed

out that as an action for breach of trust
could not possibly be brought against anybody who was not a Trustee there were no
Statutes of Limitation which, under this
sub-section, a Trustee could enjoy. See
the observation of Lord Justice Fry in *in
re Bowden*, 45 Ch. Div., 448.

If this criticism is just, the common-
law Chancellor and Chancery practitioner,
in their first shot, at all events, only fired
a blank cartridge. However, there is a
sub-section (*b*), which is as follows :—

" If the action or other proceeding is brought to
recover money or other property and is one to
which no existing Statute of Limitations applies,
the Trustee or person claiming through him shall
be entitled to the benefit of and be at liberty to
plead the lapse of time as a bar to such action or
other proceeding in the like manner and to the
like extent as if the claim had been against him
in an action of debt for money had and received,
but so nevertheless that the statute shall run
against a married woman entitled in possession for
her separate use, whether with or without a
restraint upon anticipation, but shall not begin to

run against any beneficiary unless and until the interest of such beneficiary shall be an interest in possession."

This is intelligible, and full effect has been given to it by the judges, and it now therefore may be taken as certain that whenever what I have called an honest breach of trust has been committed (for we have yet to consider the exceptions), the passage of six years will, as against anybody who has been throughout that period entitled in possession, bar the remedy of the *cestui que* trust.

The exceptions must now be stated, they are as follows :—

    1.—Where the claim is founded upon any fraud or fraudulent breach of trust to which the Trustee was party or privy, or

    2.—Where the claim is to recover trust property, or the proceeds thereof, still retained by the Trustee, or which has been

3.—Previously received by the Trustee and *converted* to his use.

These exceptions seem to explain themselves.

Any fraud or fraudulent breaches of trust are outside the statute, no one wishes to protect rogues. If the Trustee *still* has in his pocket trust funds, the fact that they have been there a long time cannot give him any right to retain them against the person whose property they really are. See and consider *Thorne* v. *Heard* (1894), 1 Chy., 599. And if the Trustee has received the money and converted it to his own use, here again the fact that he has chosen to alter the character of the property cannot give him any equity to retain it.

Upon this last exception I may refer to the case of *in re Gurney, Mason* v. *Mercer* (1893), 1 Ch., 590, merely for the purpose of quoting the language of Mr. Justice Romer. In that case two Trustees

had made, in the year 1878, an investment on mortgage said to be improper,
and the money advanced by the Trustees
to the mortgagor was paid to the mortgagor's account with the bank of which
one of the Trustees was a partner, and
was applied by the bank in reduction of
the mortgagor's debt to the bank. The
action was brought more than six years
after the date of the investment, but the
plaintiff sought to get out of the statute
by the argument that the Trustee, who
was a partner in the bank, had converted
the money to his own use. But Mr.
Justice Romer held that it would be a
perversion of the language used in the
section if he were to hold that such a
transaction as that, *being an honest
transaction*, was to be treated as a conversion to his use by the Trustee who
happened to be a partner in the bank, of
the money lent on mortgage.

One of the first cases under the statute

was the case already referred to, of *in re Bowden*, 45 Ch. Div., 444, which was an action brought against a former Trustee and the representatives of two deceased Trustees, to compel them to make good losses arising from investments negligently made on insufficient security more than six years before the action. Lord Justice Fry said that in his opinion the defendant had a good defence under the 8th Section of the Act, Sub-section (b), and added : " If this had been an action for debt, for money had and received, and the debt had arisen more than six years ago and no acknowledgment had taken place in the meanwhile, the lapse of time would have furnished a defence." And he dismissed the action with costs.

Another case may be mentioned, for it illustrates very well the utility of the Act of 1888, and its wide-reaching effect. I mean the case of *Swain* v. *Bringeman* (1891), 3 Ch., 233. In that case the

Trustees of a farmer's will, instead of
realising the residuary personalty as they
were bound to do, allowed the testator's
widow to reside on the farm carried on
by the testator, and themselves carried
on the farm, maintaining the widow
and the children out of the profits until
the youngest child attained twenty-one,
when the residuary personalty and the
realty were sold.

The result of this course of conduct
was an alleged loss of £1,800, and two of
the sons sought to make the surviving
executor and Trustee liable.

The argument for the plaintiff proceeded
on the view that according to the true
construction of the will the interest of the
plaintiffs was for legacies charged upon
land, and that accordingly there was a
Statute of Limitations applicable to such
an action, namely the Real Property
Limitation Act, 1874, Section 8, which
substitutes a period of twelve years for a

period of twenty, which was necessary
under the former Statute 3 and 4, Will
IV., Cap. 27, Sec. 40. But Mr. Justice
Romer was of opinion that the action was
not one for a legacy but for relief in
respect of a breach of trust, and that as
more than six (though less than twelve)
years had elapsed since the loss occasioned
by the breach of trust had occurred, Sub-
section (b) of Section 8 of the Trustee Act
1888, applied, and that accordingly the
action could not be sustained.

Again in 1892 a case arose in which the
section was held to apply, *in re Page*
Jones v. *Morgan* (1893), 1 Ch., 304. In
that case an infant was entitled to the
residue of the estate of a testatrix which
was to be held by the Trustees of the will
in trust for him, and to be paid to him, on
his attaining twenty-one. The testatrix
died in May 1875. The infant attained
twenty-one in December 1880, and in May
1892 he took out a summons against the

two Trustees and executors, claiming an order for the administration of the estate.

One of the defendants did not appear, and the other deposed that he had expended the whole residue during the plaintiff's minority in maintaining and educating him. He admitted that he had never rendered any account to the plaintiff, but said that he had told him during his minority how the fund had been applied. The plaintiff did not allege that the defendant had been party or privy to any fraud, or fraudulent breach of trust, and there was no evidence that the defendant had converted any part of the trust fund to his own use, or that he retained any part of it. Mr. Justice North held that the Act applied, and he dismissed the summons.

I will only refer to one other case upon this section—that of *Somerset* v. *Earl Poulett* (1894), 1 Ch., 231—a case which has been already referred to for another purpose.

But before referring to this case, and in order to make it intelligible, I must say a word about how debts can be taken out of the Statutes of Limitation by *acknowledgment.*

This law arose on the common law side under the Statutes of Limitation ; for notwithstanding the express words of those statutes, the judges soon held that an acknowledgment of a debt by the debtor within six years of action took the case out of the operation of the rule, and they admitted (until prevented by statute) parol evidence of such acknowledgment. Lord Tenterden's Act 9, Geo. IV., Cap. 14, Sec. 1, required acknowledgments to be in writing. This statute merely altered the mode of proof, and left the nature and effect of an acknowledgment untouched. See *Darby and Bosanquets' Statutes of Limitation*, 2nd Ed., page 66.

The common law cases on the subject are well worth reading as proofs of refine-

ment and subtle distinction. Some
judges based the theory of acknowledgment on a new promise to pay. Others
held that no more was required than an
admission of the existence of the debt
even though that admission were accompanied by a point blank refusal to pay, or
a claim to the benefit of the statute.
This view was justified on the ground that
Statutes of Limitation were founded on a
presumption of payment arising from
lapse of time, and as an admission of
non-payment got rid of that presumption
the statute could not apply. However,
ever since *Tanner* v. *Smart*, 6 Barn and
Cress, 603 (a decision of Lord Tenterden's),
it has been settled law that upon a
general acknowledgment where nothing
is said to prevent it, a general promise to
pay may, and ought to be, implied, but
where the party guards his acknowledgment and accompanies it with
an express statement to prevent any

such implication no such promise can be implied.

Now that Statutes of Limitation apply to express trusts, the rules of law as to acknowledgments become material, and if a Trustee who had been guilty of an honest breach of trust was ever ill-advised enough to admit in writing his obligation to make good the loss, he would thereby deprive himself of the benefit of the plea of the statute until a fresh six years had run from the date of the admission.

Returning now to *Somerset* v. *Poulett.* In that case, in 1878, the Trustees of a settlement committed an innocent breach of trust by investing the trust money upon mortgage of property of insufficient value. The mortgagor paid the interest on the money advanced direct to the tenant for life until 1890. In 1892 the tenant for life and remaindermen brought an action against the Trustees to compel

them to make good the amount of the
investment.   It was conceded that so far
as the infant plaintiffs were concerned,
the Trustees were liable to make good the
loss to the estate, but it was held by the
Court of Appeal affirming the decision of
Mr. Justice Kekewich, that the right of
action by the tenant for life against the
Trustees was barred after six years from
the time when the investment was made,
and that although the *payment of interest*
by the mortgagor direct to the tenant for
life amounted in law to a payment by
the mortgagor to the Trustees, and by
them to the tenant for life, *such payment
was not an admission or acknowledgment
which would take the case out of the
statute.*

This is a decision of great value to
Trustees; for had it been held that payment of interest on an improper investment by the Trustees to the tenant for life,
and the taking of a receipt from him, was

an acknowledgment within the statute,
Trustees would very rarely in the case of
an improper investment have been able
to avail themselves of this defence, and,
as we have already seen, improper investments are amongst the most usual of
honest breaches of trust. The judges in
deciding in the way they did, relied upon
some common law authorities, one of
which, *Morgan* v. *Rowlands*, in L.R. 7
Q.B., page 493, should be read, as it contains a valuable judgment of Blackburn, J.

It must always be remembered that
the time of limitation does not begin to
run until the beneficiary's interest is one
in possession; and therefore so long as
there is a tenant for life in existence the
statute can only run against him and
cannot begin to run against the persons
ultimately entitled until the tenant for
life is under the sod.

This is well illustrated by the case just
referred to of *Somerset* v. *Poulett*.

The Act, though only applicable to actions or other proceedings commenced after the 1st of January, 1890, applies to all existing trusts irrespective of their date.

It is perhaps worth remarking that by the Bankruptcy Act of 1883, the liabilities for honest breaches of trust were for the first time made provable in bankruptcy, and that an order of discharge releases the bankrupt from debts so provable; therefore bankruptcy is now one way out of an honest breach of trust.

Turning away from this subject altogether, I wish to say a word upon what is sometimes called the delegation of trusts as distinguished from the employment of agents.

A Trustee cannot properly delegate his trust. He is bound to give his beneficiaries the benefit of his mind upon every matter as it comes up concerning the trust affairs. He does not properly discharge the duty which he has assumed towards others if he allows a co-Trustee to conduct the trust business without reference to himself; but as we have already seen, particularly in our first Lecture, Trustees are entitled to employ agents to carry out trust transactions in the same way as reasonable men are accustomed to employ agents to carry out similar transactions in which they are personally interested.

As we have already seen when such agents have been employed, and when, in consequence of such employment, loss has arisen to the trust estate, the question always is, whether the agents were entrusted with the trust property either for a longer period than was necessary, or further than they ought to have been entrusted, having regard to the nature of their employment.

I only go over this ground again in

N

order to call attention to the 17th Section
of the Trustee Act of 1893, the first Sub-
section of which got rid of some very
troublesome earlier law. That Sub-section
is as follows : —

"A Trustee may appoint a solicitor to be his
agent to receive and give a discharge for any
money or valuable consideration or property
receivable by the Trustee under the trust by per-
mitting the solicitor to have the custody of
and to produce a deed containing any such
receipt as is referred to in Section 56 of the
Conveyancing and Law of Property Act, 1881,
and a Trustee shall not be chargeable with breach
of trust by reason only of his having made or concurred in making any such appointment ; and the
producing of any such deed by the solicitor shall
have the same validity and effect under the said
section as if the person appointing the solicitor
had not been a Trustee."

Prior to this enactment it had been
held by Chancery judges that it was no
part of the ordinary duty of a solicitor to
receive purchase-money belonging to his
client (the vendor), even though the

solicitor had possession of the deed of
conveyance. As a matter of fact, as all
professional men knew, nothing was more
in accordance with the ordinary practice
than for the vendor's solicitor who at-
tended the completion of the purchase
with the deed in his hands signed by his
client to receive the purchase-money.
But questions of this kind are determined
not by practitioners, but by the judges.
It therefore became the practice for the
solicitor for the vendor to be specially
authorised in writing to receive the purchase-money in those cases where the
vendor did not attend the completion.

By the 56th Section of the Conveyancing Act of 1881, purchase-money
could be safely paid to the solicitor who
actually produced the deed with a receipt
in it, or on it; but it was held subsequently to that Act by the judges of
the Appeal Court that Trustees selling
were not within the section. See *Bellamy*

and *Metropolitan Board of Works,* 24 Ch.
Div., 387.   But the sub-section I have
just quoted gets rid of that law and enables
persons buying from Trustees to pay the
purchase-money to the solicitor for the
Trustees, who produces the deed duly
executed by his clients and containing a
receipt for the purchase-money either in
the body of the deed or on the back
of it.

The other sub-sections of Section 17
must be studiously considered, and in
reading the whole statute   care   must
be taken to observe what sections are
made retrospective and what dates are
fixed in other sections for the commence-
ment of their operation.

I promised in an earlier lecture to
say a word on the subject of forgery.

Trustees have been held liable if they
pay trust funds to the wrong party,
though they have done so honestly,
relying upon the genuineness of docu-

ments. Thus in *Eaves* v. *Hickson*, 30
Beav., 136, Trustees paid over the trust
fund to wrong persons, trusting to a
marriage certificate which turned out to
be a forgery and were made responsible
for so doing to the extent to which the
trust fund could not be recovered from
those who had wrongfully received it.
The Master of the Rolls said :—

"This is a very hard case on the Trustees, who
were deceived by the forgery of the date in the
marriage certificate, which had been altered in a
manner which deceived them and would have
deceived any one who was not looking out for
forgery or fraud. The question is, where a
forgery is committed and a person wrongfully gets
trust money which cannot be recovered from him,
on whom is the loss to fall? I am of opinion that
it falls on the person who paid the money. Here
the loss falls on the Trustees, and the persons to
whom the fund really belongs are not to be de-
prived of it. The Trustee is bound to pay the
trust fund to the right person."

This still seems to be the law, and it
exposes Trustees to an unreasonable

amount of peril. If the fraud practised upon them is one which probably would not have escaped detection by reasonably prudent men in the conduct of their own affairs, it seems hard and contrary to the principle of *in re Belchier* and *Speight* v. *Gaunt* that Trustees should be made personally responsible for a perfectly honest and not unreasonable mistake.

In bringing these Lectures to a conclusion I will only observe that it is not at all surprising to find that just when the law of Trustees has been substantially ameliorated and their liabilities greatly reduced there should be a demand for the abolition of private Trustees altogether; and for the appointment of official Trustees to take upon themselves the administration of the wills and settlements of the country. This is the ordinary course in human affairs. Revolutions succeed periods of partial reform. It is no part of my duty to consider the wisdom or folly of so vast a proposal, but this much may I think be safely said, that so long as people are to be found willing to assume the office and undertake the liabilities of Trustees, there is no prospect of the law I have sought partially to expound becoming obsolete.

By the recent Act 59, 60 Vic. C. 35 which comes into operation (as to this part of it) on the 1st of May 1897, the High Court may in its discretion appoint a Judicial Trustee to act either alone or with any other person in trust either actually existing or about to be created. Such Judicial Trustee may be remunerated.

THE END